A Bibliographic Guide

to the Literature of

Contemporary American Poetry,

1970-1975

Phillis Gershator

The Scarecrow Press, Inc.

Metuchen, N.J.   1976

Library of Congress Cataloging in Publication Data

Gershator, Phillis.
    A bibliographic guide to the literature of contem-
porary American poetry, 1970-1975.

    Includes indexes.
    1. American poetry--20th century--History and
criticism--Bibliography. 2. American poetry--20th
century--Bibliography. I. Title.
Z1231.P7G47 [PS325]   016.811'5'4   76-41812
ISBN 0-8108-0987-7

dedicated to Anne Kelly

who inspired this project

CONTENTS

PREFACE

This is intended to be the most comprehensive and inclusive bibliography on the literature of contemporary American poetry now available; the books listed bear copyright dates of 1970 through 1975. Each title has reference to North American poetry of the present period and/or poets writing today. The titles were selected from publishers' and dealers' catalogs, periodicals, book exhibits, reference works, and the resources of the New York and Brooklyn Public Libraries. For titles I had difficulty locating, the publishers were kind enough to provide either review copies, catalog copy, or front matter. Titles for which I could not obtain adequate information or confirmation were omitted.

The book is divided into five sections. The first four--reference sources, critical and other works (excluding monographs on individual poets), anthologies, and textbooks-- are prefaced by a few words on the scope of coverage and some trends in the area. If the annotations are not based on first-hand inspection, the source of information is given. The last section provides some degree of topical access to the books listed and author and title indexes.

All the titles are interesting in one way or another, even if only as grist for opposing tendencies in poetry and poetics. Fortunately for everyone concerned, annotations and one individual's viewpoint cannot entirely take the place of personal review for whatever purposes the potential reader has in mind. My purpose here has been to provide information (author, complete title, publisher, copyright date, number of pages, and illustrative matter) for the many titles in the field, along with remarks regarding scope and theme. Teachers, students, librarians, writers, and anyone who has need of a bibliographic reference tool or desires an overview of what is being written and published in contemporary American poetry will, I hope, find this listing useful.

I am indebted to Anne Kelly, Professor of Library Science at Pratt Institute, for her support, and to David Gershator, poet and teacher, whose expertise in the field was a great help.

Phillis Gershator

PART 1

REFERENCE WORKS

Many books are obviously useful as reference sources. The following are reference works in a specific sense: bibliographies, indexes, biographies, directories, dictionaries, and encyclopedic "companions" which point the way to sources of information and/or answer ready-reference questions. Though this guide only includes books,* various organizations publish newsletters and directories, and many literary magazines include news, reviews, and up-to-date information on the poets they print. Some of the basic references --A Directory of American Poets and International Who's Who in Poetry--cite these sources. They also provide lists of audiovisual materials, as does Dudley Randall's The Black Poets. Additional information on recordings of modern poetry can be found in Miller Williams' Contemporary Poetry in America; David Morse's Grandfather Rock; and Volume 4 of the Chicorel Index to Poetry in Collections in Print, on Discs and Tapes, as well as in a number of textbooks.

Several recent (and revised) bibliographies of American literature indicate standard reference tools and significant monographs in the area of contemporary poetry. A. Robert Rodgers' The Humanities: A Selective Guide to In-

---

*Titles mentioned without bibliographic information in the paragraphs are cited fully in the other sections. Titles which appear semi-annually or quarterly are not included.

formation Sources (Littleton, Colorado: Libraries Unlimited,
1974) is a recent work including basic titles in the field. Intended as a library science textbook, it also provides a good
reference sources checklist (often annotated) for poetry in the
section titled "Language and Literature. " The discussion of
trends in modern poetry is not helpful, however, other than
listing the titles of some important works and mentioning the
names of a number of poets. Many of the titles listed in
Rodgers' guide are included here, with special emphasis on
their approaches to contemporary American poetry.

Another, less standard, guide to information sources
is The Living Z: A Guide to the Literature of the Counter-
Culture, the Alternative Press, and Little Magazines, by
Noel Peattie (1975, available for $2. 00 from Margins/Tom
Montag, 2912 N. Hackett, Milwaukee, Wisconsin 53211). It
is a collection of lists plus selected titles divided into six
sections: directories, bibliographies, periodicals about the
publishing scene, specialty lists, histories and bibliographic
essays, and how-to books in small press publishing. Checklists are appended to each section and the work is indexed.
Poetry is particularly important in the alternative press scene,
and this guide is a good starting point for those interested in
the field.

The fourth revised edition of The Literary History of
the United States, edited by Robert E. Spiller and others
(New York: Macmillan, 1974), briefly reviews in its bibliography volume major reference works in poetry published in
1970 and earlier, and lists bibliographies for individual authors including modern poets Robert Lowell, Richard Wilbur,
and others. The history volume has a new four-chapter section titled "Mid-Century and After. " The poetry chapter by
Daniel Hoffman concisely surveys the post-war scene. The

author touches on the major attitudes to form and subject ex-
pressed in contemporary poetry and concludes with mention of
poets belonging to no easily identifiable movement. Each
volume is indexed.

A seemingly exhaustive work, though in need of updat-
ing, is Charles H. Nilon's Bibliography of Bibliographies in
American Literature (New York: Bowker, 1970). It is divided into four sections--basic, author, genre (including
poetry), and ancillary bibliographies--subdivided into fairly
specific sections. Citations are nearly always arranged
alphabetically by author's name and the work is indexed.

Other bibliographies include the fourth revised edition
of Howard Mumford Jones' and Richard M. Ludwig's Guide to
American Literature and Its Backgrounds Since 1890 (Cambridge, Mass.: Harvard University Press, 1972), which provides two checklists of some important titles in the field of
modern poetry. John L. Marsh compiled A Student's Bibliography of American Literature (Dubuque, Iowa: Kendall/
Hunt, 1971), a selective list with three subheadings under
poetry: history, special studies, and 19 individual poets--
some of them modern--arranged alphabetically. The book is
easy to use but not especially helpful for contemporary poetry
beyond a few basic works. Inglis R. Bell and Jennifer Gal-
lup put together A Reference Guide to English, American and
Canadian Literature: An Annotated Checklist of Bibliographical and Other Reference Materials (Vancouver: University
of British Columbia Press, 1971). It is a student's bibliography which provides explanatory information on the basic
reference tools cited and lists several titles under the poetry
sections. Clarence Gohdes' Bibliographical Guide to the
Study of the Literature of the U.S.A., third revised edition
(Durham, N.C.: Duke University Press, 1970), is intended

for use by teachers, students, and librarians and includes a
separate listing for poetry--more extensive than some of the
other bibliographies but already dated.

Two standard bibliographies in their fifth editions are
Selective Bibliography for the Study of English and American
Literature by Richard D. Altick and Andrew Wright (New York:
Macmillan, 1975) and A Concise Bibliography for Students of
English by Arthur G. Kennedy and Donald B. Sands, revised
by William E. Colburn (Stanford, Calif. : Stanford University
Press, 1972). The Selective Bibliography is a highly selected
list of 586 items which is aimed at graduate students and
scholars so they can be their own reference librarians. It's
a compact, easy to use bibliography. A Concise Bibliography
is intended for advanced undergraduate and graduate students
in English and offers "a list of older works of demonstrated
usefulness to the student and new works that show great prom-
ise. " Books devoted to less than three authors are excluded. The well-indexed guide is divided into three parts: the
literature, the book, and the profession. The arrangement
is chronological by date of publication within various catego-
ries--Poetry and The Modern Period, for example.

Two bibliographies providing access to articles on
contemporary poets and poetry are Lewis Leary's Articles on
American Literature: 1950-1967 (Durham, N.C. : Duke University Press, 1970) and David E. Pownall's Articles on
Twentieth Century Literature: An Annotated Bibliography:
1954-1970 (New York: Kraus-Thomson, 1973--). The former
lists items appearing in a quarterly checklist of "Articles on
American Literature Appearing in Current Periodicals" in A-
merican Literature from January 1951 through January 1968,
in addition to many from other sources. The core of Articles
on Twentieth Century Literature is based on "Current Bibliog-

raphy" in Twentieth Century Literature; English language articles predominate, but articles in the major European languages are also annotated, and book reviews, popular journa-
lism, and elementary level articles on teaching literature are
excluded. The authors who are included lived and published
works in this century and are arranged alphabetically by name
or by title of the specific work being studied. The annotations are initialed. It is to be a 16-volume work, each volume covering a portion of the alphabet; thus far only a few
volumes have been published.

Four annual bibliographies in the field of literature
contain citations and/or reviews of books and articles on
modern poetry. The Modern Language Association of America published the MLA International Bibliography (New York:
Kraus, 1921--) and the Modern Humanities Research Association publishes the Annual Bibliography of English Language
and Literature (Cambridge: Cambridge University Press,
1921--); both works should be consulted though the coverage
often overlaps.

The Year's Work in English Studies, edited by Geoffrey Harlow (London: Published for the English Association
by John Murray, 1921--), is an assembling of bibliographic
essays by professors which critically describe the significant
books and articles in various areas of English studies for
the year indicated (and holdovers from the year before). The
areas of interest for work on contemporary American poetry
are the first and last sections: "Literary History and Criticism: General Works" and "American Literature: The
Twentieth Century." As with most annuals, publication lags
two years behind the material reviewed. Year's Work is well
indexed.

American Literary Scholarship: An Annual, edited by

J. Albert Robbins (Durham, N.C.: Duke University Press,
1963--), is an indexed, critical guide to current worthy studies on American literature. The signed bibliographic essays
cover, in Part I, works on individual writers and, in Part II,
periods and genres. The section on "Poetry: The 1930's to
the Present" offers a general look at the quantity and quality
of material, new journals, and significant books and articles
on poetics and individual poets.

The book reviews from Library Journal have been
bound in an annual volume titled The Library Journal Book
Review (New York: Bowker, 1967--). The section on Poetry
covers the publications of small and large publishers--largely
works by individual poets--and offers brief, informative, opin-
ionated but trustworthy signed reviews. Most are written by
librarians and professors, with their institutional affiliations
indicated. The bibliographic citation includes price and LC
number, and the titles are arranged alphabetically by author's
name.

Two of the more recent bibliographies in Black literature are Afro-American Writers compiled by Darwin T. Tur-
ner--one of the Goldentree Bibliographies in Language and
Literature (New York: Appleton Century Crofts, 1970)--and
Black American Poetry Since 1944: A Preliminary Checklist,
compiled by Frank Deodene and William P. French (Chatham,
N.J.: Chatham Bookseller, 1971). The former is a selective bibliography intended for graduate and advanced undergraduate students of literature. It is a guide to drama, fiction, and poetry by Afro-Americans and to scholarly work
about these authors. Asterisks indicate works of special importance; background references in art, music, and sociology
are also provided. Black American Poetry Since 1944 is a
list of first editions "of all separately published books and

pamphlets of poetry (excluding broadsides and leaflets of fewer than five pages) by black authors born or living in the United States, published from 1944 through the Spring of 1971" (p. 3). The arrangement is alphabetical by author, and some foreign-born poets (with note as to birthplace) are included, as are anthologies devoted to modern Black American poetry. Entries include, whenever possible, author, title, place, publisher, date, pagination, and binding.

Contemporary American Poetry: A Checklist by Lloyd Davis and Robert Irwin (Metuchen, N.J.: Scarecrow Press, 1975) is a useful "guide to American poetry of the 1950's and 60's, what has become known as 'contemporary' or 'postmodern' poetry," plus "earlier works by poets born after 1900 who remained productive after 1950" (p. iii). Authors are listed alphabetically, with their books of poetry arranged chronologically by date of publication; the cut-off date is December 31, 1973. The checklist contains a title index.

Among poetry indexes, Granger's Index to Poetry [sixth edition edited by William James Smith (New York: Columbia University Press, 1973)] is the standard reference. This edition has an expanded subject index and increasingly represents avant-garde and Black poetry. Over 500 volumes of anthologized poetry, including 114 new volumes, are indexed.

John E. and Sara W. Brewton with G. Meredith Blackburn III edit the Index to Poetry for Children and Young People: 1964-1969 (New York: H. W. Wilson, 1972). It is "a title, subject, author and first line index to poetry in collection for children and young people" which indexes 117 collections published from 1964 through 1969. A few of the many uses for this index are described in the introduction.

The Index of American Periodical Verse, edited by Sander W. Zulauf and Irwin H. Weiser (Metuchen, N.J.:

Scarecrow, 1973--), is an annual index to poetry appearing
in a significant number of periodicals. With a growing number of poet entries and periodicals in each volume (171 periodicals in the latest volume, published in 1975), the index
reflects "what is being written--and read and published--in
America today" (p. vii, first volume). Poets and translators
are listed alphabetically; a title index is included. There's
a two-year time lag between the year's work indexed and publication date.

Index to Black Poetry by Dorothy H. Chapman (Boston:
G. K. Hall, 1974) indexes 94 books and pamphlets and 33 anthologies by title and first line, author, and subject of poem
(sample headings: Africa, Beauty, Liberty). Some of the
works indexed were published as recently as 1972, and works
by non-Blacks dealing with the Black experience are included.

The computerized Chicorel Index Series includes the
four-volume Chicorel Index to Poetry in Anthologies and Collections in Print (New York: Chicorel Library, 1974). It is
not as up to date as the date of publication would indicate but
provides multiple access points in a dictionary arrangement
for 250,000 entries from works in print. There is a subject
guide for period, style, country, theme, etc. and lists of
collections, translators, authors, and publishers. The Chicorel Index to Poetry in Collections in Print, on Discs and
Tapes: Poetry on Discs, Tapes and Cassettes (New York:
Chicorel Library, 1972) is a dictionary arrangement of over
20,000 entries of poetry read on discs, tapes, cartridges and
cassettes from about 700 currently available collections of
recorded poetry on over 1,800 discs and tapes. The poetry
dates from antiquity to the present. Seven index sections
provide access by subject, performer, title, etc. In the field
of contemporary poetry, it may be easier and more rewarding

to check the less cumbersome and more current checklists and acquisition tools. These comprehensive indexes, volumes 5 and 4 respectively, are edited by Marietta Chicorel.

An Index to Criticisms of British and American Poetry, compiled by Gloria Stark Cline and Jeffrey A. Baker (Metuchen, N. J. : Scarecrow, 1973), includes material on 105 living poets and attempts to cover as much as possible from the 60's on Black poetry. Many important periodicals from 1960 through 1970 are indexed.

Contemporary Literary Criticism, edited by Carolyn Riley (Detroit: Gale Research, 1973--), is a recently initiated companion to Contemporary Authors: A Bio-Bibliographical Guide to Current Authors and Their Works edited by Clare D. Kinsman (1962--, semi-annual). In these ongoing encyclopedias of current criticism, the critical passages quoted were written during the past 25 years on writers now living and those who have died since January 1, 1960. About 200 authors are listed alphabetically in each volume with an average of five excerpts from critical articles or reviews for each. The excerpts are taken from about 250 books and several hundred issues of about 50 magazines. This is a very useful, time-saving work with many contemporary poets included in an international selection. Each volume has to be consulted for new material on both new and previously listed authors. Volumes 2 and 3 are cumulatively indexed.

Among the directories in the field, Contemporary Poets of the English Language, edited by Rosalie Murphy and James Vinson (Chicago: St. James Press, 1970), also includes concise, signed critical commentary on about 300 particularly outstanding poets "as well as those about whom critical comment is often difficult to obtain" (p. xi). It is an essential, enlightening volume with biographical and bibliographi-

cal information for 1100 poets now writing in the English
language who were selected on the advice of critics and
editors.   The work includes notes on the advisors, contributors, and consultants and provides a list of anthologies
since 1960 that include contemporary poetry.   The second edition (New York: St. Martin's Press, 1975) includes fewer
poets (about 800) with a signed critical essay on each and an
appendix of entries on major post-war poets who have died.

The International Who's Who in Poetry: 1972-73, third
edition edited by Ernest Kay (London, 1972), is a good source
for biographies and bibliographies of a large number of American poets, though the slant of the work is English.   The information in the more than 3,000 entries includes personal
data, occupation, organizational membership, awards, address,
etc.   The volume also includes: poems from the International Who's Who in Poetry Awards, a portrait gallery of prize
winners and Poets Laureate of the U. K. and U. S., articles
on poetry societies, society directories, directory of little
magazines, poetry publishers in Britain and the U. S., lists
of prizes and awards, and poetry on records and tapes.

Poets & Writers, Inc. publishes a useful and inexpen-
sive directory--available from the Publishing Center, 27 West
53 Street, New York, N. Y.   10019, for $6.00.   A Directory
of American Poets (New York: Poets & Writers, 1973--)
comes out annually and is intended "to aid groups and individuals interested in locating and sponsoring contemporary A-
merican poets and writers....   Poets who have published re-
currently in little magazines are eligible for listing."   The
1975 edition provides the following information for over 1,500
poets: current address, telephone numbers, work preference,
languages spoken, most recent book.   The entries are arranged alphabetically by state of residence with an additional al-

phabetical listing of the names included, and lists of writers
with special ethnic backgrounds are given. An adminis-
trators' listing of names and addresses of over 450 organizations that have sponsored poetry readings and workshops is
also arranged by state. The work concludes with lists of
contemporary anthologies, audiovisual materials, references
and addresses, bookstores, and a checklist to guide organi-
zers of readings and workshops.

The Writers Directory: 1971-73, edited by A. G.
Seaton (Chicago: St. James, 1971), is not the first place one
would look for information on poets, but it does include an
international group of poets for whom addresses, publications,
appointments, and nature of writing are given. The Writers
Directory: 1974-76 (New York: St. Martin's Press, 1973)
"lists more than 18,000 living writers in English"; "each en-
try indicates other reference works in which biographical or
bibliographical details may be found" (publisher).

Four recent ethnic directories have appeared, partly
necessitated by the exclusion of Black and Puerto Rican
writers from the standard directories. Ann Allen Shockley
and Sue P. Chandler regard Living Black American Authors:
A Biographical Directory (New York: Bowker, 1973) as a
pioneering venture. The work is based on research and questionnaires. Occupation, birth, education, family, member-
ships, awards, publications, mailing address are given; the
work includes a list of Black publishers and a title index.

Broadside Authors and Artists: An Illustrated Biographical Directory (Detroit: Broadside Press, 1974), edited
by Leaonead Pack Bailey, is based mainly on questionnaires
sent to authors and artists published by Broadside Press and
the Heritage Series edited by Paul Breman. Entries include
a small photo, personal data, address, education, politics,

religion, awards, writings, and remarks by the author. Out
of the 192 entries, 90% are not listed in Contemporary Authors.

Black American Writers Past and Present: A Biographical and Bibliographical Dictionary by Theressa Gunnels
Rush, Carol Fairbanks Myers, and Esther Spring Arata (Metuchen, N. J. : Scarecrow, 1975) is a highly recommended
source for bio-bibliographical information on Black writers.
Information for each poet includes a listing of all known published books and, for the major poets, biographical data or
references to the information in standard directories, appear-
ances in anthologies and periodicals, and citations for selected reviews and critical pieces. In some cases, photos and
interjections--pithy quotations on writing, life, Blackness,
etc. --are provided. The work includes a 60-page bibliography
and partial listing of critics, historians, and editors.

Puerto Rican Authors: A Biobibliographic Handbook
by Marnesba D. Hill and Harold B. Schleifer with translations
by Daniel Maratos (Methuchen, N. J. : Scarecrow, 1974) is a
"bilingual annotated biobibliographic guide to the history and
literature of Puerto Rico by Puerto Rican writers from 1493
to the present ... intended as a convenient working tool" for
college and secondary school libraries and urban public libraries in Spanish speaking communities. (p. v). The work
is arranged alphabetically by author with topical, chronological and title indexes. The introduction by María Teresa Ba-
bín is an essay titled "Literature and Life in Puerto Rican
Culture. " There are 20 entries for poets from the last three
decades, eight of whom were born in the 1920's and early
30's. References to younger Puerto Rican poets will have to
be found elsewhere. A Directory of American Poets and three
anthologies--Nuyorican Poetry, From the Belly of the Shark,

and The Puerto Rican Poets/Los Poetas Puertorriqueños--
would be helpful in this respect.

A vital directory for practicing poets and others is the
International Directory of Little Magazines and Small Presses
edited by Len Fulton (Paradise, Calif.: Dustbooks, 1964--),
an annual publication covering everything you ever wanted to
know but couldn't find out about small magazines and presses
--from acquisition to submitting material for possible publication. It's an alphabetical listing by title and/or name of
press with the following information: editor(s), address, material used, editorial comments, frequency of appearance,
subscription and individual prices, founding year, pages, size,
circulation, production method, length of reporting time of
submissions, payment, ad rates, discounts, back issue prices,
number of issues/titles published and expected, and membership in organizations. Dustbooks also publishes the Directory
of Small Magazine/Press Editors and Publishers (Paradise,
Calif.: Dustbooks, 1970--). Names are listed alphabetically
with name and address of periodical or press, reading preferences, influences, and reasons for editing.

The Whole Cosmep Catalog edited by Dick Higgins
(Paradise, Calif.: Dustbooks, 1973) is already a classic.
It's a "one time supplement to the Directory of Little Magazines and Small Presses," listing COSMEP members with
their addresses. Each member designed a page to represent
itself--from the staid to freaky--with reproductions of draw-
ings, poetry, and catalog lists. Len Fulton discusses small
press publishing and the origins of COSMEP in the introduction. Aside from factual information, the catalog visually
preserves the range of styles in small press publishing.

The American Center of P.E.N. publishes an annual
List of Grants and Awards Available to American Writers

which is available from the center at 156 Fifth Avenue, New
York, N.Y. 10010, for $1.00 for members, $2 for nonmem-
bers. The directories listed here and other writers' directories also provide this kind of information.

As for special dictionaries in the field, Babette
Deutsch's Poetry Handbook: A Dictionary of Terms, fourth
edition (New York: Funk & Wagnalls, 1974), is the basic
work and one of the more enjoyable dictionaries to read--well
written and illustrated with quotations. The poets cited are
indexed. Many poetry textbooks also contain more or less
ample glossaries. One in particular, Lewis Turco's Poetry:
An Introduction Through Writing, revolves around definitions
and examples.

Crowell's Handbook of Contemporary American Poetry:
A Critical Handbook of American Poetry Since 1940 by Karl
Malkoff (New York: Crowell, 1973) is the only "companion"-
type volume that focuses specifically on the topic at hand.
The introduction--"A Short History of Contemporary American
Poetry"--"traces the development of the aesthetic theories of
major schools (or movements) in contemporary American poetry; it explores the assumptions underlying the poets' methods
... and it identifies the poets most commonly associated with
those movements" (p. vii). The book includes over 70 alphabetically arranged essays·on movements and individual poets
which contain biographical statements, descriptions of the
poet's principal themes, methods, school, and development,
a close reading of specific poems, and bibliographies of the
poet's work. It is an attempt to be representative and to
examine, rather than evaluate, American poets who have not
commercially published books of poetry before 1940--a basic
reference providing useful background information and com-

pact, sympathetic coverage of many major modern poets.

The enlarged edition of the Princeton Encyclopedia of Poetry and Poetics, edited by Alex Preminger, Frank J. Warnke, and O. B. Hardison, Jr. (Princeton, N.J.: Princeton University Press, 1974), covers a broad range of topics with long initialed entries, many including bibliographies, and shorter entries with examples illustrating terms such as Cacophony and Dimeter. This valuable standard reference work treats "all aspects of its subject"--history, movements, critical philosophy; for example, in this edition there are entries for Rock Lyric, Computer Poetry, Black Poetry in the U.S., Puerto Rican Poetry, Metacriticism, and so on.

The illustrated Concise Encyclopedia of English and American Poets, edited by Stephen Spender and Donald A. Hall (London: Hutchinson, 1970, 2nd revised edition), contains initialed entries on general topics and nearly 300 poets. The work treats English and American poetry from the beginning of the language to the present and is suitable for the general reader and secondary school student. Bibliographies, an index of poets quoted, a general index, and notes on the contributors are included.

There are several literature companions of wider scope, and the Penguin Companion to American Literature, edited by Malcolm Bradbury, Eric Mottram, and Jean Franco (New York: McGraw-Hill, 1971), is one of the better ones. The initialed, bibliographic entries are arranged alphabetically and divided geographically into two sections: U.S.A. and Latin America. The volume provides "broad coverage of the most important names in American writing from the early period of settlement through to the immediate present, including figures of historical as well as directly literary interest"; popular figures, influential American thinkers, and important

publications are included as well as "a small number of subject entries designed to suggest important features of American literary thought and experience" (p. 11). The entries
reflect personal and critical judgments and a British perspective. The emphasis is on the twentieth century; many contemporary poets are included, though many others are not.
Basic selected bibliographies are given for the two sections.

      Many poetry anthologies have reference value. Some
of the revised and updated editions of earlier anthologies have
become authoritative in their way; for titles see The Literary
History of the United States, A Directory of American Poets,
and Contemporary Poets of the English Language. The new
Norton Anthology of Modern Poetry is an essential reference
volume--vast, comprehensive, with supplementary bibliographies, biographies, criticism, and history. Over 150 other anthologies are listed in Section III.

PART 2

THE LITERATURE ON
CONTEMPORARY AMERICAN POETRY

Histories, collections of essays, interviews, and theoretical, critical and expository works dealing with more than
three poets each are included in this section--the literature
of contemporary American poetry. It is a large field and
there are no neat boundaries. Many comprehensive works
on literature include statements about contemporary poetry
and some of these have been listed, but I have tried, in the
main, to include only those works where the discussion is
very significant. In selecting titles for this section, I had
to rely somewhat on intuition: books dealing specifically with
American poetry of earlier periods were omitted, yet books
dealing philosophically with poetry in general were included if
they had possible relevance for someone interested in a broad-
er look at the topic.

A discussion of literary criticism is too large a subject to go into here. It is, in fact, a whole field in itself,
and, according to poets, an important one. Broadside Press,
for example, is consciously building a body of criticism of
Black poetry. Critical reaction indicates that a work is being
taken seriously. It is feedback. It is publicity. Criticism
can enhance and articulate one's initial reactions, promote
understanding, and reflect on implications.

The interview technique is old, but now that the question and answer format has taken over the best seller lists it fits right in--and the collections of interviews are as informative and entertaining as you would expect. The histories, covering varying lengths of time, provide an overview and an introduction. Some are biased and personal; others attempt neutrality. Many of the works include anthologies of their own and/or quote extensively from poetry in part or whole.

The push to publish, according to American Literary Scholarship: An Annual/1972, has resulted in much unoriginal, graceless, insignificant work. Collections of essays, reviews, and critical pieces are one way to survey the publication of literary journals and small magazines without searching and sifting and, at least, to get a feel for the way poetry criticism is handled, who is considered, and what is important to some of the arbiters of taste in our culture.

ALLEN, Donald M. and Tallman, Warren, eds. The Poetics of the New American Poetry. New York: Grove, 1973. 463 pp.
    Collection of previously published articles, essays, manifestos, and letters by 22 American poets (plus Lorca and D. H. Lawrence) dealing with the art of poetry. The poets represented are "seeking a new or re-newed writing in hopes of a new or re-newed world" (p. ix). The collection, beginning with Whitman's letter to Ralph Waldo Emerson and concluding with a piece by Philip Whalen written especially for this book, is arranged by author in a loosely chronological pattern. A basic source book providing theoretical alternatives to the views of Brooks, Tate, Ransom, etc., with very brief chronology of significant books, periodicals, and presses from 1909-1973. A companion to Allen's anthology The New American Poetry: 1945-1960 (New York: Grove, 1960).

ANDERSON, Douglas. My Sister Looks Like a Pear: Awakening the Poetry in Young People. New York: Hart, 1974. 268 pp.

Well written, inspirational book by a writer with the
Poets in the Schools program. It includes 250 creative pieces
by students, practical advice on teaching creative writing, and
some of the author's personal experiences with the program
and the students. Index of titles and first lines.

BELL, Bernard W. The Folk Roots of Contemporary Afro-
American Poetry. (Broadside Critics series: James A.
Emanuel, general editor) Detroit: Broadside, 1974.
80 pp.
In thesis style the author discusses Johann Herder's
theory of folk art and its indirect influence on W. E. B. Dubois, Alain Locke and James Weldon Johnson, "the elder
statesmen of the Harlem Renaissance of the Twenties," and
Richard Wright, Ralph Ellison and Jones/Baraka, "the spiritual fathers of the Black Arts Movement of the Sixties" (p.
20). The work is an attempt to lend scholarly weight to critical analyses of Black poetry by emphasizing the ideological
and cultural roots and, therefore, the respectability, legiti-
macy and value of this poetry. Much is obvious and much
is a striving for connections that may or may not exist, but
the community and vitality of Black art is self-evident and in-
forms even the style of the final chapter--"Contemporary
Afro-American Poetry as Folk Art," a straightforward look
at individual poets. References and bibliography.

BLOOM, Harold. The Anxiety of Influence: A Theory of
Poetry. New York: Oxford University Press, 1973.
157 pp.
"A theory of poetry by way of a description of poetic
influence, or the story of intra-poetic relationships ..." with
two corrective aims: "to: de-idealize our accepted accounts
of how one poet helps to form another ... to try to provide
a poetics that will foster a more adequate practical criticism"
(p. 5). Truly creative criticism and poetics using a variety
of styles and forms (including poetry) to work through "six
revisionary ratios as mechanisms of defense" in "a unified
meditation of the creative mind's desperate insistence upon
priority" (p. 13).

_____. A Map of Misreading. New York: Oxford Uni-
versity Press, 1975. 206 pp.
Described in The New York Times Book Review
(April 13, 1975) as brilliant, revisionist, extravagant, poetic
theory which deepens and extends the vision set forth in The
Anxiety of Influence, a vision of "Oedipal ravagement, pathos
and psychological drama" providing "an inner plot for poetry."

BOGAN, Louise. A Poet's Alphabet: Reflections on the Lit-
    erary Art and Vocation. New York: McGraw-Hill, 1970.
    474 pp.
        Collection of criticism, mostly of pieces from The
New Yorker, written during the last 20 years and ranging
widely in time and place. The author was not sympathetic to
modern poetry (The Year's Work in English Studies: Vol.
52, 1971, p. 433).

BOYD, Gertrude A. Teaching Poetry in the Elementary
    School. Columbus, Ohio: Merrill, 1973. 105 pp.
        "Gives specific information on how and when poetry
can be used most effectively in the classroom" (publisher).
Chapter headings: Why Poetry for Children, The "How" of
Reading Poetry, The "What" and "When" of Reading Poetry,
Song and Verse--Prelude to Poetry, Art of Memorizing, The
Writing of Poetry, A Place for Everything (audiovisual ma-
terials, etc.). Bibliography.

BOYERS, Robert, ed. Contemporary Poetry in America:
    Essays and Interviews. New York: Schocken Books,
    1974. 368 pp. Illustrated with six drawings.
        Twenty-four articles, interviews, and critical essays
on poets and topics such as "The New Surrealism" written
from a variety of perspectives. The collection is representative but leans to some poetry considered "old fashioned" or
"literally splendid. " It is based on the Spring-Summer 1973
issue of Salmagundi, later expanded for teachers and students
interested in the current scene who "wish to develop a critical apparatus for dealing with the work of a variety of poets"
(p. vii). Notes on contributors.

BROOKS, Cleanth. A Shaping Joy: Studies in the Writer's
    Craft. New York: Harcourt Brace Jovanovich, 1971.
    393 pp.
        Essays containing "observations on the role of the
poet, the uses of metaphor, and formalist criticism... " (A-
merican Literary Scholarship: An Annual: 1972, p. 334).

BROOKS, Gwendolyn and others. A Capsule Course in Black
    Poetry Writing. Detroit: Broadside Press, 1975. 64 pp.
        Suggestions--ideological and practical--by Gwendolyn
Brooks, Keorapetse Kgositsile, Haki R. Madhubuti (Don L.
Lee), and Dudley Randall. Bibliographies, questions common-
ly asked Dudley Randall, and sample worksheets.

BRUCHAC, Joseph. The Poetry of Pop. Paradise, Calif. :
    Dustbooks, 1973.

  'It is time that the lyrics of the best popular songs were looked at in the way we look at the best poems." The author/editor/poet discusses Dylan, The Doors, The Stones, Ochs, Prine, and others (publisher).

BRUNS, Gerald L. Modern Poetry and the Idea of Language: A Critical and Historical Study. New Haven, Conn. : Yale University Press, 1974. 300 pp.
  An academic study of language and poetics approached linguistically, rather than a study of modern poetry, intended for students of literature. Its purpose is to inquire into "antithetical conceptions of poetic or literary language": the "hermetic" and "orphic." References, notes, index.

BUCHLER, Justus. The Main of Light: On the Concept of Poetry. New York: Oxford University Press, 1974. 183 pp.
  A philosophical approach to an understanding of "the nature of poetry." The first four chapters deal with sterile and "unaccountably persistent ideas and allegiances"; the last three attempt to construct "a just theory of poetry" (p. 4). "Chapter V provides for poetry an elemental location, a terrain. Chapter VI ['Ontological Parity and the Sense of Prevalence'] formulates traits ... to differentiate the poetic product from any other" (p. 5). The last chapter considers "Knowledge, Actuality and Analysis in Poetry."

BURNSHAW, Stanley. The Seamless Web: Language-Thinking, Creature-Knowledge, Art-Experience. New York: Braziller, 1970. 320 pp.
  "Poetry begins with the body and ends with the body .... My approach, then, is 'physiological' ... " (p. 1). Poetry is an "art experience" which the author views with reference to the forces of the human mind--"primal" and "civilized," "voluntary" and "involuntary." An original and provocative (if not concise) exploration in three parts based on literary, physiological, and psychological analyses of artistic creativity and the audience reaction to it. References, notes, and index.

CARGAS, Harry J. Daniel Berrigan and Contemporary Protest Poetry. New Haven, Conn. : College and University Press, 1972. 126 pp.
  Sympathetically critical essays examining six "protest" poets: Richard Eberhart, Karl Shapiro, Robert Lowell, Allen Ginsberg, Jones/Baraka, and Daniel Berrigan. Index and references.

CHARTERS, Samuel. Some Poems/Poets: Studies in American Underground Poetry Since 1945. Berkeley: Oyez,
   1971. 118+ pp. Photos of eight poets by Ann Charters.
      "Loose responses to some of the implications" of the
non-academic poetry of the last 20 years. Personal, elegant
collection of essays on Spicer, Duncan, Brother Antoninus,
Larry Eigner, Ginsberg, Ferlinghetti, Lew Welch, Olson,
Creeley, and Snyder.

CHATFIELD, Hale. Building an Audience for Poetry. Ashland, Ohio: Ashland Poetry Press, 1970.
      "A pamphlet for those who would develop among young
people an interest in poetry as a lively art" (publisher).

CREELEY, Robert. A Quick Graph: Collected Notes and Essays. San Francisco: Four Seasons Foundation, 1970.
   365 pp.
      Collection of pieces from underground and small press
publications. Sections include critical essays on Olson, Duncan, and Dorn, art and prose, and poetry in general expressing the concerns of non-academic poets (The Year's Work in
English Studies: Vol. 52, 1971, pp. 433-4).

CURRY, Andrew. Bringing Forth Forms. Paradise, Calif. :
   Dustbooks, 1973.
      An editor/poet/teacher's "philosophical memoirs, es-
says on language, poetry, mythology, the treatment of schizo-
phrenia, and the nature of meaning" (publisher).

DEMBO, L. S. and PONDRON, Cyrena N. , eds. The Contemporary Writer: Interviews with Sixteen Novelists and Poets. Madison: University of Wisconsin Press, 1972.
   296 pp.
      Analytically oriented interviews which first appeared
in the journal Contemporary Literature. The eight poets in-
terviewed are James Merrill, Kenneth Rexroth, Gwendolyn
Brooks, George Barker, and the "Objectivist" poets George
Oppen, Carl Rakosi, Charles Reznikoff, and Louis Zukofsky.
Index.

DICKEY, James. Sorties. Garden City, N. Y. : Doubleday,
   1971. 227 pp.
      Part I, about two-thirds of the book, consists of
self-conscious journal jottings. Part II: several essays on
poetry and poets which seem to have been previously published.

DODSWORTH, Martin, ed. The Survival of Poetry: A Con-

temporary Survey. London: Faber & Faber, 1970.
256 pp.
      The English and American poets represented in the
seven essays by the editor and five other British writer/crit-
ics seem "to be the poets of the present day, that is, who
have found their style in the post-war world, who are most
aware ... of the social and historical context in which they
write" (p. 30). The American poets considered in these critical surveys are Robert Lowell, John Berryman, Sylvia Plath,
and the Black Mountain Poets--Charles Olson and Edward
Dorn. The book contains some elegant and/or acerbic criticism expressing a strong point of view. The editor deals
"academic" poetry a blow in the introduction and claims that
neither the well-made nor the translatable poem has much to
offer the serious poet. Among the Americans, James Dickey,
Robert Bly, and James Wright are his targets. Twenty-one-
page bibliography.

DONOGHUE, Denis, ed. Seven American Poets from Mac-
      Leish to Nemerov: An Introduction. Minneapolis: Uni-
      versity of Minnesota Press, 1975. 329 pp.
      "Essays on MacLeish, Eberhart, Roethke, Jarrell,
Berryman, Lowell, Nemerov by such critics as Grover Smith,
M. L. Rosenthal, and Ralph J. Mills, Jr." (publisher). The
essays are "competent ... professional ... valuable as surveys, and in many instances they are truly illuminating" (Library Journal, July 1975, p. 1324). Bibliography and index.

DURR, R. A. Poetic Vision and the Psychedelic Experience.
      Syracuse, N.Y.: Syracuse University Press, 1970.
      275 pp.
      "... Not attempting an all-inclusive analysis of the
psychedelic experience but speculating upon its correspondence
with one great kind of literature (pp. ix-x) ... the primary
task of this essay is to demonstrate that the psychedelic experience and romantic, mystical, or visionary literature do
indeed have in common much that is essential" (p. xii).
"... This book might serve as a sort of selection, with run-
ning commentary, of literary passages bearing upon the psychedelic issue ... not set forth as a thorough, logical dis-
course on its subject, but rather as a series of quotations in
organized juxtaposition tending toward the representation of a
view and a style or life" (p. xiv). The author makes connections of interest to writers and students of contemporary (any)
poetry, though the poetic examples he uses are largely from
the 19th century. The book is even more "mind expanding"
for those not already familiar with the work of Aldous Huxley,

Watts, Suzuki and others from which the author has drawn.
References, bibliography, and index.

FEDER, Lillian. Ancient Myth in Modern Poetry. Prince-
    ton, N.J.: Princeton University Press, 1971. 432 pp.
    "The aim of this book is twofold: to develop a
definition of myth as a continuous and evolving mode of expression, and to indicate how classical myth functions in modern English and American poetry as an aesthetic device
which reaches into the deepest layers of personal, religious,
social, and political life. I believe that such an approach
elucidates the nature of myth as a key to unconscious mental
processes and, at the same time, reveals some of the essential themes, symbols, and techniques of twentieth-century poetry" (p. vii). The study focuses on Yeats, Pound, Eliot,
and Auden with reference to the writings of Freud, Jung,
Frazer, Vico, and Spengler. The last chapter touches on
several other modern poets, including Lowell, Plath, Ginsberg, and Corso, who have "employed classical myth in
modes such as confessional and Beat poetry that, on the sur-
face, seem unsuited to its traditional associations" (p. 407),
and W. S. Merwin, for whom "myth is his most important
and powerful vehicle in defining the role of the poet in the
present" (p. 412). References and index.

FISCHER, Barbara. Poetry Self-Taught. North Babylon,
    N.Y.: J. Mark Press, 1972.
    Chapters on poetic techniques and the printing, pro-
motion, and selling of poetry (publisher).

FOX, Hugh. The Living Underground: A Critical Overview.
    Troy, N.Y.: Whitston, 1970. 161 pp.
    Twelve essays on individual poets--Levy, Miller,
Higgins, Blazek, Wagner, Cauble, Simon, Deutsch, Kryss,
Morris, and Potts--follow an introductory survey of the Underground poetry scene. The author concludes with a comparison between the Beats and Hippies and a description of the
Underground poets as witnesses to change--"sensors" reporting change--influenced, for better and worse, by the culture
for which they are trying to create alternatives. A good
follow-up to Charters' Some Poems/Poets, which deals with
poets who already have Aboveground reputations.

FULLER, Roy. Owls and Artificers: Oxford Lectures on
    Poetry. New York: The Library Press, 1971. 136 pp.
    Six perceptive lectures given in 1969-70 when Roy
Fuller was Professor of Poetry at Oxford University. The

topics include revolutionary and sentimental poetry, artifice,
Wallace Stevens, explications and misreadings of poetry, and
taste. Index.

_____. Professors & Gods: Last Oxford Lectures on Po-
etry. New York: St. Martin's Press, 1973. 176 pp.
Nine lectures (following the six in Owls and Artificers) presented at Oxford.

GIBSON, Donald B. , ed. Modern Black Poets: A Collection
of Critical Essays. (Twentieth Century Views series)
Englewood Cliffs, N. J. : Prentice-Hall, 1973. 181 pp.
Thirteen previously unpublished and published essays
in the first collection of critical essays on Black poetry. The
last six are concerned with contemporary poets--Robert Hayden, Jones/Baraka, Don L. Lee, Sonia Sanchez, and Nikki
Giovanni--and the topics humanistic protest and black hate.
Notes on contributors and 15-page selected bibliography.

GINSBERG, Allen. Allen Verbatim: Lectures on Poetry,
Politics, Consciousness. Edited by Gordon Ball. New
York: McGraw-Hill, 1974. 269 pp.
A "collection of transcribed talks given by Allen Ginsberg on a tour of colleges he made in 1971.... The core of
his book is his personal credo, his ideas about the relations
of experience to its 'natural' expression, his elaborations upon
the ways formalism of any sort inhibits or destroys spontan-
eity" (The New York Times Book Review, March 2, 1975,
p. 4).

GOODMAN, Paul. Speaking and Language: Defense of Poetry.
New York: Random, 1972. 242 pp.
Surveys theories of language, describes process of
writing, defines audience for poetry, and surveys the topic
of organic form (American Literary Scholarship: An Annual:
1972, p. 333).

GRAFF, Gerald. Poetic Statements and Critical Dogma.
Evanston, Ill. : Northwestern University Press, 1970.
189 pp.
A revised 1962 doctoral dissertation with a duel aim:
"to demonstrate the unfortunate- theoretical and practical con-
sequences of several types of antipropositional theories; and
secondly to outline a poetics which finds a place for the propositional and assertive element in poetry and yet also does
justice to the contemporary emphasis upon organic unity and
experiential complexity uniquely achieved in poetry" (p. xiii).

The first four chapters deal with representative contemporary
theorists and the last two argue "the case that propositional
assertion and expository argument are important semantic and
structural principles of poetry ..." (p. xv). References and
index.

GRAHAM, John. Craft So Hard to Learn: Conversations
    with Poets and Novelists about the Teaching of Writing.
    George Garrett, editor. New York: Morrow, 1972.
    94 pp.
        Eleven interviews in question and answer format deal-
with the teaching, craft and art of creative writing. The interviews were taped for John Graham's radio program, "The
Scholar's Bookshelf," during the Hollings Conference in Creative Writing and Cinema in June, 1970. The conversations
are arranged in chronological order and each is preceded by
a biographical note and bibliography of works. The poet/
teachers included are Henry Taylor, Richard Wilbur, James
Seay, James Whitehead, and James Dickey. They express
some sharp opinions, though the depth of the exchanges is
limited by the media aspect--conversational and off the cuff,
with the interviewer, John Graham, doing a good proportion
of the talking.

_____. The Writer's Voice: Conversations with Contem-
    porary Writers. George Garrett, editor. New York:
    Morrow, 1973. 294 pp.
        More interviews with the same poets plus others.
Same arrangement and biobibliographical information, though
the emphasis is on the poet's own work and the work of
others rather than teaching.

GUTTMAN, Allen. The Jewish Writer in America: Assimi-
    lation and the Crisis of Identity. New York: Oxford Uni-
    versity Press, 1971. 256 pp.
        "This book is a study of the responses of Orthodox
and other Jews in an unfamiliar country that combined new
freedoms with more than a trace of old hostilities" (p. 11).
It is a sociological, historical approach to literature. The
modern poets the author discusses somewhat cursorily are
Karl Shapiro, Irving Feldman, John Hollander, and Allen
Ginsberg as he examines their references to Jewish/American
themes. The exclusion principle he uses permits the omission
of many noted Jewish poets because they do not explicitly deal
with these themes. But also not considered are younger poets who do deal extensively with Jewish references. The author, in trying to reach a middle ground between superficial-

ity and depth, produces a discussion which isn't completely
satisfying. He suggests, however, areas for speculation con-
cerning identification with life-style rather than religion, mar-
ginality and double alienation and its effects on creativity, and
the fact that "Jewish literature" now depends on an irreverent
generation. References, a supplementary bibliography, and
index.

HAMILTON, Anne. The Seven Principles of Poetry. Boston:
    The Writer, 1970. 298 pp.
    They are inspiration, intuition, imagination, content,
rhythm, form, and expression. A clear textbook-like job intended for individual study or class work.

HAMILTON, Ian. A Poetry Chronicle: Essays and Reviews.
    New York: Barnes and Noble, 1973. 175 pp.
    "A comprehensive view of what has been happening
in poetry in recent years by one of the most important and
consistently interesting critics of contemporary poetry. Includes assessments of the work of MacNeice, Lowell, Berryman, Larkin, and Fuller" (publisher).

HARROWER, Molly. The Therapy of Poetry. (American
    Lecture Series. Editor: Molly Harrower) Springfield,
    Ill.: Charles C. Thomas, 1972. 117 pp.
    "The theme of this book is not so much that poetry
can be used in formal therapy, but rather that poetry is
'therapy' and is part and parcel of normal development"
(p. 3). The author treats the chronological development of
poetic expression from pre-schooler to adult, using her own
poetry and notebooks as material on which to explicate. It
is a peculiar exercise in self-analysis, and the observations
might have been better presented as concise statement. References.

HASSAN, Ihab. Contemporary American Literature: 1945-
    1972: An Introduction. New York: Frederick Ungar,
    1973. 194 pp.
    A review of fiction, poetry, and drama. The section
on poetry includes an introduction and a discussion of Lowell
("Major Poet") and "Prominent Poets" Theodore Roethke, John
Berryman, and Allen Ginsberg, followed by "Types and Trends
of Poetry" broken down into seven topics: Variations on
Formalism; the Black Mountain Poets; The San Francisco Poets; Beats, Nature Mystics, and Others; The New York Poets;
The Post-Romantics; The Black Poets. The poetry scene is
handled with enthusiasm (in the present tense) and touches on

many poets and schools--a compact book fulfilling its function
as an introduction.   Index of authors and a bibliography.

HEIDEGGER, Martin. Poetry, Language, Thought. Trans-
    lations and Introduction by Albert Hofstadter. New York:
    Harper, 1971.   229 pp.
        Seven pieces from various works written between
1935 and 1960 relating poetry, art, thought, and language to
Being.   "Poetry--together with the language and thinking that
belong to it and are identical with it as essential poetry--has
for Heidegger an indispensable function for human life: It is
the creative sources of the humanness of the dwelling life of
man.   Without the poetic element in our own being, and without our poets and their great poetry, we would be brutes, or
what is worse and what we are most like today: vicious auto-
mata of self-will" (p. xv).

HENDERSON, Stephen.   Understanding the New Black Poetry:
    Black Speech and Black Music as Poetic References.
    (An Institute of the Black World book) New York: Mor-
    row, 1973.   394 pp.
        Interesting "thesis" anthology emphasizing the poetry
of the 60's and commenting in the long introduction on: what
is Black poetry, who is to judge, and how?   "These questions
can not be resolved without considering the ethnic roots of
Black poetry, which I insist are ultimately understood only
by Black people themselves" (pp. 7-8).   The author discusses
theme, structure, and speech to suggest a critical framework
for evaluating Black poetry.   The anthology is chronologically
divided into three sections--the last the most extensive, with
50 poets represented.   Biographical notes.

HOLLAND, Norman N.   Poems in Persons: An Introduction
    to the Psychoanalysis of Literature. New York: Norton,
    1973.   183 pp.
        A work divided into three parts--"A Maker's Mind,"
"Two Reader's Minds," and "My Mind and Yours"--previously
offered "separately as lectures and articles to literary and
psychoanalytic audiences" (p. x).   "I have built this book
around lyric poems and occurrences of one particular fantasy:
the unconscious wish to undo, either lovingly or hostilely,
one's separateness from a nurturing other" (p. ix).   It is an
attempt to see how subjective and objective combine when we
have experiences.   The study revolves around the poet Hilda
Doolittle (H. D.) as an illustrative example, and the reactions
of a man and woman to psychological testing and one of H.
D.'s poems.   The author develops several perceptive princi-

ples based on observation in this humanistic psychoanalytical
approach to literature.   Guide to further reading and references.

HOLLANDER, John. Vision and Resonance: Two Senses of
    the Poetic Form. New York: Oxford University Press,
    1975. 314 pp.
        "Systematically reduces poetry to craft.... In part,
Hollander wants to make 'more public ... the private insights
of the ear of a sensitive reader, ' but his means frustrate his
aim.... Hollander, whatever his prosaic stiffness, is a valuable critic" (The New York Times Book Review, August 3,
1975, pp. 17-18).

HOPKINS, Lee Bennett. Pass the Poetry, Please! Using
    Poetry in Pre-Kindergarten-Six Classrooms. New York:
    Citation Press, 1972. 199 pp. Illustrated.
        An informative and useful book for teachers contain-
ing, in addition to techniques for encouraging children to write
poetry, biographies of children's poets (Aileen Fisher, Langston Hughes, Eve Merriam, etc.), poetry in media, and bibliographies of poetry in paperback and poetry written by children. Author and title indexes.

KAMINSKY, Marc. What's Inside You It Shines Out of You.
    New York: Horizon Press, 1974. 236 pp.
        A book combining case history, instructional tech-
niques, self-searching, parables, dialogs, and poetry, rising
out of the poetry groups which the author conducted as a
group worker with the Jewish Association for Services for the
Aged.   The first two sections describe the people, sessions,
and techniques involved and include samples of the work produced.   The third section consists entirely of poetry, some
of it remarkable.   What's Inside You will do for poetry and
older adults what Kenneth Koch's Wishes, Lies, and Dreams
did for kids.

KOCH, Kenneth. Rose Where Did You Get That Red? Teach-
    ing Great Poetry to Children. New York: Random House,
    1973. 360 pp.
        The author introduces his elementary school students
to great adult poetry by making it a part of their own writing.
In the introduction he describes his technique, class plan, attitudes.   In the sections titled "Ten Lessons," each chapter
consists of a poem, an explication of its "poetry ideas" and
the techniques used to teach and inspire the children, whose
own poems follow each explication.   An anthology of about

60 poems, with suggestions for teaching each, is included.
Poems by children from Swaziland conclude the book. Required reading for anyone involved in poetry and/or creative
education. Author and Title Index of Adult Poems. Subject
Index of Adult Poems.

_____ . Wishes, Lies, and Dreams: Teaching Children
    to Write Poetry. New York: Vintage, Random House,
    1970. 309 pp. Illustrated with black and white photos.
    The first chapter surveys ideas and techniques the
author/poet used for eliciting poetry from children without
the restrictive use of rhyme and meter. The following 20
chapters are made up of collections of poetry by the students
of P. S. 61 in N. Y. C. ; notes on the idea or technique used
conclude each group--"Lies, " "Sestinas, " "Metaphors, " etc.
Already a classic in the field. Required reading for those
working creatively with children.

LACEY, Paul A. The Inner War: Forms and Themes in
    Recent American Poetry. Philadelphia: Fortress Press,
    1972. 132 pp.
    A six-chapter work addressing itself to five poets--
James Wright, William Everson (Brother Antoninus), Robert
Bly, Denise Levertov, and Anne Sexton--and two questions:
"What have contemporary poets to say about the spiritual
state of our world, what kind of critique of our culture does
their work offer and how might it throw light on similar problems being examined by theologians and religious thinkers?"
and "What are the relations of form to content in contemporary American poetry? (p. 1). Upbeat criticism mainly interesting for its emphasis on religious content and imagery
and approach to the poetic process, e. g. , Sexton's "sacra-
ment of confession. "

LARRICK, Nancy, ed. Somebody Turned on a Tap in These
    Kids: Poetry and Young People Today. New York: De-
    lacorte, 1971. 178 pp.
    Reasons behind the youthful surge toward poetry and
teachers' experiences are described in eleven papers and discussions rising out of the Poetry Festival sponsored by Le-
high University's School of Education in 1969. Poets, anthol-
ogists, teachers, and students participated. The text includes
examples of poetry written for and by kids (the latter is
good).

LEE, Don L. Dynamite Voices I: Black Poets of the 1960's.
    (Broadside Critics Series: James A. Emanuel, general

editor) Detroit: Broadside Press, 1971. 92 pp.
      According to the general editor, "the series is an
attempt to introduce a fairly uniform body of sustained criticism into the tradition of black poetry ...a response to the
need of Black people for respectful, honest evaluations written by and for members of their own race" (p. 11). This
volume is a personal overview by a participant who discusses
the Black critic, Black writing and publishing, tradition and,
critically and briefly, fourteen poets of the 60's (and 70's).
Selected bibliography of Afro-American poetry published in
19 60-70 including broadsides, anthologies and tapes.

LEEDY, Jack J. , ed.   Poetry the Healer.   Philadelphia:
      Lippincott, 1973.   220 pp.
      Ten essays and case histories dealing with the use
of poetry as therapy by doctors, teachers, and writers. The
articles include examples of poetry written by convicts, drug
addicts, the handicapped and disturbed. A rewarding follow-
up to the editor's Poetry Therapy (Philadelphia: Lippincott,
19 69). References and index.

LEVERTOV, Denise.   The Poet in the World.   New York:
      New Directions, 1973.   275 pp.
      In the preface, the author persuasively describes her
reasons for gathering 31 previously published prose pieces
into this collection. The five sections deal with fiction, writing and inspiration, and teaching, other writers, and "Life
at War. " An essential collection by an important poet.
Indexed.

LIVINGSTON, Myra Cohn.   When You Are Alone /It Keeps You
      Capone: An Approach to Creative Writing with Children.
      New York: Atheneum, 1973.   238 pp.
      Intends to answer the teacher's question, "Where do
I start when I teach creative writing?" Suggestions for stim-
ulating creativity, observations on the work produced, and
critiques of some accepted methods of teaching poetry. Examples of children's work are included.

LOPATE, Phillip.   Being with Children.   New York: Double-
      day, 1975.
      "Clearly one of the best books on 'getting' children
to write. Lopate, who worked through the Teachers and
Writers Collaborative at P. S. 90, New York City, records
both the internal and external politics of an artist negotiating
cognitive and affective change in a static institution... " (Library Journal, October 15, 1975, p. 1918).

McGOVERN, Robert. A Poetry Ritual for Grammar Schools. Ashland, Ohio: Ashland Poetry Press, 1974.
An "approach to developing and maintaining an interest in poetry among elementary pupils. Provides ... a beginning anthology of mature poetry ... and suggests source material for use in the classroom and for the teacher's individual study" (publisher).

MAJOR, Clarence. The Dark and Feeling: Reflections on Black American Writers and Their Works. New York: Third Press, 1974. 153 pp.
Nineteen thoughtful essays, interviews, letters, and reviews, about two-thirds of which were published previously. The author/poet includes several articles on contemporary Black poetry.

MAZZARO, Jerome, ed. Modern American Poetry: Essays in Criticism. New York: McKay, 1970. 368 pp.
Collection of essays (some previously published) on fifteen well known and established poets, chronologically arranged from Walt Whitman to W. D. Snodgrass, expressing a range of critical points of view.

MERSMANN, James F. Out of the Vietnam Vortex: A Study of Poets and Poetry Against the War. Kansas: University Press of Kansas, 1974. 277 pp.
"A thematic analysis of the poetry written during the 1960's in protest of the American War in Vietnam. " A work of scholarship and criticism "and perhaps the best single study of contemporary poetry now available" (Choice, November 1974, p. 1309). Focuses on the works of Ginsberg, Bly, Levertov, and Robert Duncan. Indexed and documented.

MILES, Josephine. Poetry and Change: Donne, Milton, Wordsworth, and the Equilibrium of the Present. Berkeley: University of California Press, 1974. 243 pp.
"In the first two chapters of this book I relate present concepts of parts and wholes in their linguistic and artistic structures and in their assumption of linguistic and artistic norms. In the third, with borrowings and adaptations of tables and text from earlier work, I relate both individual and group to temporal development by the agreements and variations they maintain in language. The following chapters, on individuals and eras, attempt to make certain specific illustrations of how such relations work, in the eccentricity or adaptability of a writer to his time, with some sense for the present of where we are moving" (p. 5). The last three

chapters, under the heading "Present Values," discuss Donne's
influence on 20th-century English poetry, examples of vocabu-
lary usage by modern poets, and generalizations based "upon
the books of poems published in America and received by the
Massachusetts Review in 1965 and 1970 and upon an analysis
of the chief words, measures, and structures in books of
poems published in the 1960's and 1970's by ten poets born
since 1930" (p. 172): Jones, Kelly, McClure, Rothenberg,
Snyder, Sward, Anderson, Mathews, Tate, and Cruz. The
impression is one of catalogs and lists with little ideological
thrust, though the book did receive the James Russell Lowell
Prize.

MILLER, Marcia Muth. How to Write and Sell Your Poetry.
    Santa Fe, New Mexico: Sunstone Press, 1974. 33 pp.
        The most obvious and set up questions, but there
may be people out there who need them answered (with that
extra little bit of sunshine and reassurance).

MILLS, Ralph J., Jr. Cry of the Human: Essays on Con-
    temporary American Poetry. Urbana, Ill: University of
    Illinois Press, 1975. 275 pp.
        The preliminary essay, "Creation's Very Self: On
the Personal Element in Recent American Poetry," touches on
major contemporary poets who wish "to speak to us, without
impediment, from the deep center of a personal engagement
with existence" (pp. 6-7). In the following essays on Roethke,
Ignatow, Kinnell, Donald Hall, and Philip Levine, the author
covers each poet's work as an "enthusiastic commentator."
Bibliography and index.

NEMEROV, Howard. Reflexions on Poetry & Poetics. New
    Brunswick, N.J.: Rutgers University Press, 1972.
    233 pp.
        Twenty-six essays (24 of which were previously pub-
lished) divided into six sections. Part I contains three essays
exploring "some internal and constructive aspects of lyric
poems, such as metaphor and the humble enough comparison
of poems with jokes" (p. viii). Part II "is about a number
of authors I care for" (p. viii); Part III an essay on Blake
and Wordsworth; Part IV "a sort of vaudeville interlude" on
blurbs, translations, and bad reference books; Part V "about
the self poetizing" (p. xiii); and Part VI concerned with poetry and the future. Thought-provoking, sometimes scathing,
sometimes humorous, critical and self-critical work by a
"distinguished" poet (an adjective Nemerov trounces and probably thought he had laid to rest in the essay title "The Lan-

guage of Praise: A Review of Some of Our Most Distinguished Recent Blurbs"!). Unfortunately, dates for some of the
essays are not given, nor are the publication dates of the
books he reviews.

NORRIS, Ruby Lee, ed. The Turtlie and the Teacher: A
     Dialog between Poets and Students. Virginia: Richmond
     Intercultural Center for the Humanities, 197?. 88 pp.
     Illustrated.
     "A partial record of the interaction between poets
and children," growing out of the Poetry-in-the Schools program. Michael Mott, Dabney Stuart and Sylvia Wilkinson are
the writers involved. Some student work is included within
the text and in the concluding anthology. Teachers will find
it enlightening. Index of poets and poems.

O'BRIEN, John, ed. Interviews with Black Writers. New
     York: Liveright, 1973. 274 pp. Photos of the writers.
     Seventeen interviews (four published previously) con-
ducted by mail, telephone, or in person and presented in
question and answer format. The emphasis is on influences,
techniques, and individual works. The interviews are prefaced by the editor's background comments describing the
writers' importance, interests, present occupations, and the
interviewing situations themselves. The younger poets included are Michael Harper, Robert Hayden, Clarence Major,
Ishmael Reed, Alice Walker, and Al Young. The editor's
introduction is a brief, general discussion of Black literature
and critical fallacies about Black literature. He advocates
dealing with writers as writers rather than pigeon-holing them
into the literary establishment's conception of blackness.
Bibliography.

OLSON, Charles. Poetry and Truth: The Beloit Lectures
     and Poems. Transcribed and edited by George F. But-
     terick. San Francisco: Four Seasons Foundation, 1971.
     75 pp.
     Lectures given at Beloit College during the week of
March 25, 1968. Disjointed comments punctuated by readings
from his poetry. Introduction by Chad Walsh. Notes.

OWEN, Guy, ed. Modern American Poetry: Essays in Crit-
     icism. Deland, Fla.: Everett/Edwards, 1972. 266 pp.
     Seventeen critical essays (some by poets) on poets
ranging from Edwin Arlington Robinson to James Dickey.
All but two of the essays were previously published and most
were written in the 1960's. "The essays should add up, so

far as possible, to a complete history of what is significant
in American poetry since World War I," though there is, the
editor also writes, "a Southern bias in the [highly personal]
collection" (p. xii). The editor's concluding essay, "Post-
script: American Poetry in the 60's," relates to contemporary poetry in a personal, critical, often negative way. It
should be pointed out that Kenneth Koch is not dead and that
Donald Allen's The New American Poetry: 1945-1960 can
hardly be called notorious. The author concludes that "poetry in the 60's is neither moribund nor tranquilized--though
it does lack the rowdy excitement of the 20's, American poetry is merely waiting for the next breakthrough" (p. 262).
Notes on contributors are included in a volume intended for
the "undergraduate or lay reader interested in poetry" (p. xii).

PACKARD, William, ed. The Craft of Poetry: Interviews
    from the 'New York Quarterly. " Garden City, N. Y. :
    Doubleday, 1974. 340 pp.
        In the introduction, the editor discusses interviewing
technique, content, and procedure, and the questions asked
in a typical New York Quarterly interview. A group of reg-
ulars, individually or together, interviews 17 poets including Erica Jong, Diane Wakoski, and Robert Creeley. Photographs and selected bibliographies are included for each poet.

PAINTER, Helen W. Poetry and Children. Newark, Del. :
    International Reading Association, 1970. 104 pp.
        "Reviews technical aspects of poetry and literary
terms, and offers realistic teaching suggestions with samples
which appeal to contemporary interests of pupils" (publisher).
Bibliography.

PAZ, Octavio. The Bow and the Lyre (El Arco y La Lira):
    The Poem, The Poetic Revelation, Poetry and History.
    Translation by Ruth L. C. Simms. (The Texas Pan
    American Series) Austin, Tex. : University of Texas
    Press, 1973. 281 pp.
        Translation from the second edition (1967) of the au-
thor's wide-ranging philosophical essays dealing with three
questions: 'Is there a poetic utterance--the poem--irreducible
to any other form of expression? What do poems say? How
is the poetic utterance communicated?" (p. 15). Appendices,
index.

PENDLEBURY, B. J. The Art of the Rhyme. New York:
    Scribner's, 1971. 116 pp.
        "The contention elaborated in the various chapters of

this book is that rhyme ... has an important function to ful-
fill in tightening stress-patterns, giving definition to stanza-
forms, and so intensifying the emotional quality of a poem"
(p. 5). Not comprehensive nor particularly historical but an
attempt to show rhyme's importance and relevance to the
achievements of many poets. One of the seven chapters is
titled "Rhyme in Modern Poetry." Several suggestions for
reading or reference and an index.

PHILLIPS, Robert. The Confessional Poets. (Cross-cur-
    rents/Modern Critiques series: Harry T. Moore, gen-
    eral editor) Carbondale, Ill.: Southern Illinois Univer-
    sity Press, 1973. 173 pp.
        An introductory, sympathetic but critical approach to
Robert Lowell, W. D. Snodgrass, Anne Sexton, John Berryman, Theodore Roethke, and Sylvia Plath. "The first book-
length attempt at examining what has come to be a major development in American literature in the second half of the
twentieth century"--the age of Autobiography (p. xi). "I have
concentrated," writes the author, "on poets whose confessional books have been issued since 1959.... I have commented
on the subject of the poets' work rather than the form" (pp.
xiii-xiv). The introductory chapter reviews and defines "The
Confessional Mode in Modern American Poetry." The other
chapters deal with individual poets in the manner of an academic survey--overviews with some explication of individual
books and poems. Four of the seven chapters were published
in the 1970's in literary journals. The readers at whom this
volume is aimed would be better off going to the poetry itself, undoubtedly finding the guide unnecessary. "Confessional poets" are accessible without a great deal of subject explication. References, an index, and a selected bibliography
of works by confessional poets are included.

PIETRKIEWICZ, Jerzy. The Other Side of Silence: The Po-
    et at the Limits of Language. London: Oxford University
    Press, 1970. 128 pp.
        Philosophical discussion ranging widely and compara-
tively over international poetry in an investigation of "the poets' desire to die with poetry and the desire to go beyond the
words, and whether this means the ultimate failure of poetry
as a literary medium or whether, on the contrary, it suggests
that poetry reaches the sublime when it ceases to be a medium ... the problem is essential to the poetic condition..."
(p. 2). References and index of names.

RABAN, Jonathan. The Society of the Poem. London: Har-
    rap, 1971. 191 pp.

Concerned with the destruction of "poetic" language
after Eliot, and literature in its social context.   Sympathetic
approach to modern poetry with reference to English and
American poets including Emmett Williams, Olson, Plath, etc.
(The Year's Work in English Studies: Vol. 52, 1971, pp.
383 and 434).

RANDALL, Dudley. Broadside Memories: Poets I Have
   Known. Detroit: Broadside Press, 1975. 64 pp.
   Photos.
   Celebrates the tenth anniversary of Broadside Press
and includes program notes for the anniversary celebration,
congratulatory advertisements, samples of poetry and broadsides, and a previously published history of the press. Dudley Randall remembers Gwendolyn Brooks, Nikki Giovanni,
Etheridge Knight, Andre Lorde, Lee/Madhubuti, Sonia Sanchez.

RANSOM, John Crowe. Beating the Bushes: Selected Essays,
   1941-1970. New York: New Directions, 1972. 176 pp.
   Eleven essays, some published previously in The
Kenyon Review, arranged chronologically: eight from the
1940's, two dated 1952, and one dated 1970. The latter treats
a philosophically Hegelian approach to poetry and the author's
"homelier" conclusions: that "a poem is an organism in action," needing head, heart and feet. Today the feet--meters,
rhythms, rhymes--"do not aspire faithfully to the obligations
of reciprocity. That is the weakness of a great deal of meaningful verse in this century..." (p. 176).

RASMUSSEN, Dennis. Poetry and Truth. (De Proprietatibus
   Litterarum Series Minor, 20) The Hague: Mouton, 1974.
   123 pp.
   Originally a Ph.D. dissertation, this philosophical
discussion of poetry and its relation to propositional truth,
closure, disclosure, kitsch, fundamental speaking, and value
would be of interest to the literary critic and philosopher.
References, bibliography, and index.

REXROTH, Kenneth. American Poetry in the Twentieth Century. New York: Herder and Herder, 1971. 180 pp.
   A personal, informal history with the last of eight
chapters dealing with the post-1955 poets. Many of the lead-
ing poets of the 60's and 70's are mentioned.

RODITI, Edouard. The Disorderly Poet & Other Essays.
   (Capra Chapbook Series, No. 29) Santa Barbara, Calif.:
   Capra Press, 1975. 71 pp.
   Three essays, the first of which, "The Disorderly

Poet: Towards a Psychopathology of Artistic Creation," deals
with physiological and psychological variations (self- and drug-
induced) and their relationship to creativity. The author-poet,
who experiences temporal-lobe seizure, recounts his own
states of consciousness during an attack.

ROSENTHAL, M. L. Poetry and the Common Life. New
    York: Oxford University Press, 1974. 148 pp.
        A thematically handled, six-chapter appreciation and
explication of modern poetry emphasizing "poetry's immediacy
and relevancy" to our lives "by recalling that it is the poets,
through their constant response to the touch of life, who are
the truest spokesmen for the wide human world in which they
move and dream" (p. x) and by recognizing that "human life
... is the province of everyone's thought, not just that of
literary specialists" (p. ix). A discussion aimed primarily
at the literate but uninitiated general reader and/or teacher.
Index of quotations.

SCOTT, Nathan A. , Jr. The Wild Prayer of Longing: Po-
    etry and the Sacred. New Haven, Conn. : Yale Univer-
    sity Press, 1971. 124 pp.
        Lucidly examines "certain forms and meanings of the
poetic imagination in this century" in the work of Olson, Eberhart, Roethke, and others. Addressed "to readers with
some understanding of recent theology and poetry" (The Library Journal Book Review: 1971, p. 315). Index and bibliography.

SHAPIRO, Karl. The Poetry Wreck: Selected Essays, 1950-
    1970. New York: Random, 1975.
        The original publication and presentation dates of these
articles and lectures on individual poets and the poet in America are not given, except for "The Poetry Wreck" printed in
1970 in Library Journal. It is an attack on contemporary
students, education, literary standards, and, most especially,
Rod McKuen--a superficial article on a topic better dealt with
by Lewis Turco in Poetry: An Introduction Through Writing.
An enjoyable and revealing collection, though it travels down-
hill toward the end.

SHAW, Robert B. , ed. American Poetry Since 1960: Some
    Critical Perspectives. Cheshire, Eng. : Carcanet Press,
    1973. 220 pp.
        "A multi-focussed view of American poetry" taking
"account of many of the period's salient features... " (p. 11),
supporting, generally, the view of 60's poetry as a poetry of

revolt. Thirteen descriptive essays by poets and critics on
topics such as protest poetry and women's poetry, as well
as on individual poets. Index, notes on contributors, and
bibliography.

SHERMAN, G. W. Poet and the Flea: On Beat, Image and
    Milieu of Poetry. San Jose, Calif.: Cobra Press, 1971.
    64 pp.

SKELTON, Robin. The Poet's Calling. New York: Barnes
    & Noble, Harper, 1975. 214 pp.
        "A good book about the making of poetry and about
being a poet, written by one with all the qualifications for
speaking interestingly and authoritatively.... He uses his
own experience and that of many other poets, mostly modern,
to explore the creative process from the psychology of per-
ception to the methods of the craft" (Library Journal, Septem-
ber 1, 1975, p. 155]). Indexed.

_____. The Practice of Poetry. New York: Barnes &
    Noble, 1971. 184 pp.
        A book by the English/Canadian poet, teacher, and
critic that succeeds in combining "technical instruction in
verse craftsmanship with instruction in the manipulation of
the imagination and the development of individual poetic vision" (p. vii). Intended for young poets and teachers of writing, it has nine chapters on such topics as "Approaches to
Form" and "The Voices of Poetry," with guides in the appendix to the technology of verse, rhyme, metrical feet, stanza
forms, obsessive forms, and other verse forms.

SMITH, Ray. Permanent Fires: Reviews of Poetry, 1958-
    1973. Metuchen, N.J.: Scarecrow Press, 1975. 137 pp.
        A collection of 131 brief reviews and annotations
which appeared in Library Journal, the Minneapolis Sunday
Tribune and daily Star between 1958 and 1973. The books of
or about poetry discussed are mostly by contemporary poets
(May Sarton, Reed Whittemore, etc.), though recent translations of Darío, Villon, and others are also reviewed.
Limited in use, but it does reveal one reviewer's sensibility
at work. The appendix, "Poetry Selection and the Imagination," touches on the library emphasis poetry deserves. Index of author, title, subject.

SNYDER, Richard. Poet to Teacher to Student. Ashland,
    Ohio: Ashland Poetry Press, 1971.
        "An essay, directed toward teachers, by a practicing

poet suggesting an approach to teaching high school students
the art of poetry" (publisher).

SPEARS, Monroe K. Dionysus in the City: Modernism in
    the Twentieth Century. New York: Oxford University
    Press, 1970. 278 pp.
        Chronological examination of modernism in poetry
within its cultural setting, written in a not particularly elegant
thesis style. The author describes James Dickey, with his
strong sense of the Dionysian forces in nature, as one of the
most promising poets to emerge in the 1960's. An interesting study for those working in the area of contemporary poetry. Indexed.

_____. Space Against Time in Modern Poetry. (Mono-
    graphs in Literary Criticism, no. 2) Fort Worth: Texas
    Christian University Press, 1972. 35 pp.
        "Cecil B. Williams memorial lecture in American
Literature, 1971."

STAUFFER, Donald Barlow. A Short History of American
    Poetry. New York: Dutton, 1974. 459 pp.
        The author has tried "to provide biographical and his-
torical information ... to make connections between various
poets and periods, and to give a sense of the range of a poet's work ... but principally ... a sense of the quality of
each writer ... what makes him unique, what makes him
stand out from his contemporaries and his ancestors" (p. xvi).
"With some exceptions the book is organized around two major poets for each chapter, surrounded by a group of contemporaries" (p. xvi). The last of the twelve chapters deals with
"Some Contemporaries," concluding with a look at Denise
Levertov and Jones/Baraka. This is a conscientious, academic book though not, in its last chapter, as contemporary
as the date of publication would make it appear. Extensive
bibliographies and index.

SUTTON, Walter. American Free Verse: The Modern Revo-
    lution in Poetry. New York: New Directions, 1973.
    230 pp.
        "This book concentrates on the origins and growth of
the powerful free verse movement from its beginnings in the
Romantic revolution to the present" and discusses representative figures and groups of poets from the beginning of the 19th
century to the post-war years. Portions were previously published. The final chapter, "The Revolution Renewed: Contemporary Poetry," purposefully limits itself to a survey of

free verse in the work of Charles Olson, Denise Levertov,
Robert Duncan, the Beat poets, Sylvia Plath, John Ashberry,
Kenneth Koch, Thomas Merton, and in concrete poetry. Re-
ferences and index.

TERRY, Ann. Children's Poetry Preferences: A National
    Survey of Upper Elementary Grades. NCTE Research
    Report No. 16. , 1974. Approx. 72 pp.
        "Poems children like best are analyzed by type, con-
tent, and age using the results of a national survey to discov-
er the poetry preferences of fourth, fifth, and sixth graders.
Terry concludes that children this age have definite preferences
on which teachers can capitalize to reverse pupils' tendency
to reject poetry as they grow older. She compares the relationship between the preferred poems and the personal and
social characteristics of children in urban, suburban, and
rural schools. Implications for teaching pinpoint teacher ne-
glect of poetry in the upper elementary classroom and the
need to create an informal environment in which poetry is a
natural daily activity" (quoted from the National Council of
Teachers of English Catalog of Publications, Resources for
English and the Language Arts [1974-1975], p. 14).

TREFETHEN, Florence. Writing a Poem. Boston: The
    Writer, 1970. 219 pp.
        Intended mainly for the "motivated but relatively in-
experienced amateur poet.... It will describe the progressive
stages that go into the making of most competent poems--
planning, the actual work with language and form, appraisal
and revision--and point towards some of the problems that
writers can encounter in these stages" (p. xi). Suggested
projects are appended to each section, becoming more difficult as the book progresses. Examples of poetry by Plath,
Nemerov, Wilbur, and others serve as illustrations. Logical-
ly conceived and simply written. Useful for independent or
classroom use. Glossary.

WALDROP, Rosmarie. Against Language? 'Dissatisfaction
    with Language' as Theme and as Impulse Toward Experi-
    ments in Twentieth Century Poetry. (De Proprietatibus
    Litterarum Series Minor, 6: C. H. Van Schooneveld,
    editor). The Hague: Mouton, 1971. 132 pp.
        Systematic study of poetic technique that affects and
tries to change language--i. e. , the "devices that break rules
of language" (p. 12). "My procedure was this: after collect-
ing poems that seemed to go against the code of the languages
I tried to abstract some categories for ordering them, if only

crudely. The categories I decided on are the techniques of
disruption, negation and borrowing from other symbolic sys-
terms" (p. 14). "It turned out ... that none of the techniques
discussed are in fact alien to language.... There is an element of disruption in every metaphor: negation is implicit
in the basic linguistic operation of selection; all poems have
sound, a shape on the page, structure, and some coupling by
sound or look, and thus in a way all borrow from music, art,
mathematics, and autism" (p. 122). The examples are drawn
largely from French and German dadaist and surrealist poetry
(untranslated), but this thesis is of interest to students and
critics approaching American avant-garde poetry from a linguistic point of view. Notes, references, index, and bibliography.

WARREN, Robert Penn. Democracy and Poetry. Cambridge,
    Mass.: Harvard University Press, 1975. 102 pp.
        The 1974 Jefferson Lecture in the Humanities revised
for publication and concerned with "the interrelation of three
things: democracy, poetry (really art in general), and self-
hood" (p. xi). "A personal exploration," elegant and stimu-
lating. Notes.

WHISNANT, Charleen and Hassett, Jo. Poetry Power: Ideas
    for Creative Writing. Charlotte, N.C.: Red Clay Books,
    1973. 41 pp.
        Concise collection of suggestions for creative writing
in the schools with grade level indicated. Includes selections
from students' work and short bibliography.

_____. _____. Word Magic: How to Encourage Chil-
    dren to Write and Speak Creatively. Garden City, N.Y.:
    Doubleday, 1974. 166 pp.
        Creativity stimulating ideas plus numerous examples
of pre-school and school-age children's poetry. The book re-
peats the work of other poet-teachers (Koch, etc.) but is still
valuable for the parents and teachers for whom it is intended.

WHITLOW, Roger. Black American Literature: A Critical
    History. Chicago: Nelson, 1973. 287 pp.
        "With a 1,520-title bibliography of works written by
and about black Americans." The author surveys the works
and influences of 45 writers, by periods, beginning with the
year 1746. Sections VI and VII relate to work from 1940-
1960 and 1960 to the present and touch on specific writers.
The four poets considered in the latter section are Ishmael
Reed, Etheridge Knight, Jones/Baraka, and Nikki Giovanni.
Index.

WITUCKE, Virginia. Poetry in the Elementary School. (Literature for Children series: Pose Lamb, consulting editor) Dubuque, Iowa: Wm. C. Brown, 1970. 115 pp.
    A "starting point" to help the reader become an enthusiastic user of poetry, the book provides a "taste of poetry for children, a feeling for it, and some information about it" (p. ix). The three sections--"What Is Poetry," "Finding Poetry," and "Poets and Pedagogues"--deal concisely with such topics as evaluation, selection, non-print materials, teaching techniques, and program planning. Selected references are included for each section, as well as many examples of poetry, including children's work. A good basic reference for teacher, librarian, parent. Indexed.

WOLSCH, Robert A. Poetic Composition Through the Grades: A Language Sensitivity Program. (Practical Suggestions for Teaching: Alice Miel, editor) New York: Teachers College Press, 1970. 183 pp.
    An important and useful book for English teachers. Twelve chapters cover the field, from uncovering and recognizing the poetic process to dignifying and sharing student poetry. Samples of childrens' work and bibliographies.

WOODCOCK, George, ed. Poets and Critics: Essays from "Canadian Literature," 1966-1974. Toronto: Oxford University Press, 1974. 246 pp.
    Seventeen essays on 18 modern Canadian poets including Margaret Atwood, Eli Mandel, Leonard Cohen, etc. Not intended to be representative but "to find those happy conjunctions when a poet meets the right critic" (p. viii). The critics are themselves often poets. Ample quotations from the poetry and a chance to get acquainted with Canadian literati. Bibliographic references.

PART 3

ANTHOLOGIES

Poetry seems to speak less today to academic, esoteric interests than to popular concerns. It is often plain-talking, free-flowing, passionate, confessional, hard-hitting, and, at the same time, highly crafted and self-conscious, frequently expressing the singular vision of those who have been ignored or oppressed. Other interpretations can be drawn from the anthologies of the 70's. Plurality is a sign of life; there are probably as many interpretations as there are poets and small press publications.

Anthologies reflect past and present and, possibly, the future. A few anthologies will become landmarks. They will have defined a trend--thematic or poetic--or the selection itself will have represented a significant segment of the poetry world, if only from an important editorial viewpoint. Some anthologies convey an excitement which propels their importance into the future. Most of them today seem to fill gaps in publishing and a lag in recognition that sometimes spans centuries. Black, Puerto Rican, Indian, Chicano, gay, women's, and radical poetry appears in the anthologies of the 70's, reflecting both this lag in recognition and the efflorescence that recognition and the times encourage.

Some may question the motivation involved in compiling anthologies--money, "publish or perish," self-promotion.

Editors often include their own work. They often score personal points in their omissions and inclusions. But self-interest also demands that the editors compile collections that will be to their credit, that fill a need or otherwise make a literary contribution. And anthologies that make it to book form have to hold up, to some extent, under the editorial scrutiny of the publishers.

We pay attention to anthologies. Most individuals, teachers, librarians, etc. can't hope to acquire a truly representative selection of contemporary works by individual poets, partly because the outpouring is so huge and so difficult to trace through the usual reviewing and sales channels. Such a collection would also be beyond most private and institutional budgets. Anthologies fill the need to be representative of a variety of poets and selection criteria. They provide an overview, a sampler, or make a statement that can't be ignored (refused--maybe; ignored--no).

An anthology which gives the poems space and includes bibliographical and biographical notes on contributors is preferable. Indexes are also desirable; an anthology of lesser worth with adequate indexes may have more reference value than an intrinsically better anthology without indexes. Most hardbound editions come in paperback as well; several excellent anthologies are paperback originals.

Many anthologies have been omitted from this list in the interest of keeping within the range of a topic that overflows arbitrary boundaries. Anthologies in series like New Directions, New American Review, Intro, and The American Literary Anthology have been excluded, as have works including five contemporary poets or less. Specifically subject-oriented anthologies (including poetry from many countries and various periods) and anthologies originally published before 1970 have also been omitted.

The poetry in contemporary anthologies is often chosen
on the basis of the person writing it--skin, cultural background, sex. If personal characteristics were a basis for exclusion before, the anthologies of the 70's right that wrong.
It isn't the ideal situation, but at least now there are many
cliques, not just a few. In the 80's, perhaps, special interests will yield to human interests and compilers will pass on
the poems themselves.

ABDUL, Raoul, comp. The Magic of Black Poetry. New
    York: Dodd, Mead, 1972. 118 pp. Illustrated by Dane
    Brown.
        Poems for young readers by a wide ranging group of
black poets with several modern American poets represented.
Commentaries and notes on the contributors.

ADOFF, Arnold, ed. Black Out Loud: An Anthology of Mod-
    ern Poems by Black Americans. New York: Macmillan,
    1970. 86 pp. Illustrated.
        Attractive volume of easy-to-grasp poetry by estab-
lished and younger black poets (36) writing on a variety of
topics. Intended for younger readers. Biographical notes
and indexes to authors, titles, and first lines.

_____. It Is the Poem Singing into Your Eyes: Anthology
    of New Young Poets. New York: Harper & Row, 1971.
    128 pp. Illustrated.
        Poems by 55 young, mostly teenage, contributors.
A relatively good, socially concerned collection selected from
over 6,000 manuscripts submitted to the editor. Indexes to
the authors and their work, first lines, and titles.

_____. My Black Me: A Beginning Book of Black Poetry.
    New York: Dutton, 1974. 83 pp.
        A tasteful selection of 50 poems for children, includ-
ing work by Sam Cornish, Nikki Giovanni, Langston Hughes,
and 22 others. Indexes to authors and first lines. Notes on
the poets.

_____. The Poetry of Black America: Anthology of the
    20th Century. New York: Harper, 1973. 552 pp.
        Over 600 poems by 145 poets showing "the diversity,
the depth of Black American poetry up to its 'second renais-

sance' of today's fine young poets" (p. xvi). In her introduction, Gwendolyn Brooks applauds the anthology's inclusion of
both major and minor stars and regrets some of the exclu-
sions. Nevertheless, "he has given us impressive variety ...
the hot, broad blockbuster" (p. xxxi). The poets are arranged by date of birth from W. E. B. DuBois to Julianne Perry.
About one-third of the contributors were born in the 1940's
and 50's. The most comprehensive modern Black American
poetry anthology around, nicely balanced between basic "over-
anthologized" works and the unanthologized.

ALGARIN, Miguel and Piñero, Miguel, eds. Nuyorican Po-
    etry: An Anthology of Puerto Rican Words and Feelings.
    New York: Morrow, 1975. 185 pp. Photos by Gil
    Mendez.
         "More than a score of unevenly gifted but impassioned
young Nuyoricans are represented ... echoes the emergent
black poetry of the 60s; more original, poignant and restrained
is a group of evolutionary poems ... " (Publishers Weekly,
October 27, 1975, p. 51).

ALIX, ed. One-Eighty-Five. San Francisco: Mongrel Press,
    1973. 288 pp. Illustrated.
         Poetry, drawings, and human statements by 78 known
and unknown friends of the editor who lingered at 185 Marina,
"a gathering place during the North Beach/Haight-Ashbury
Movement of the sixties" (p. vi).

ALLEN, Terry D. , ed. Arrows Four: Prose and Poetry by
    Young American Indians. New York: Washington Square
    Press, 1974. 175 pp. Illustrated with photos.
         Poetry and prose by American Indian high school stu-
dents written in a Bureau of Indian Affairs creative writing
project, with an introduction by the editor--the director of the
project. The four sections of the book were previously pri-
vately printed as annual volumes (1969-1972). The index provides access to author, tribe, and school. The poetry is uneven and not as strong and fresh as one might expect, but
some individual poems are memorable ... and poignant.

_____. The Whispering Wind: Poetry by Young American
    Indians. Garden City, N. Y. : Doubleday, 1972. 128 pp.
         Mae Durham, in her introduction, notes that the cul-
ture is reflected but that the poets "transcend the culture,
and mirror the very stuff of life" with an "earthy and lyrical
use of language" (p. xii). The work included stems from the
Institute of Indian Arts at Santa Fe, New Mexico. Notes on

the poets describe plans for the future, background, interests, etc.

ANGOFF, Charles, and others, eds. The Diamond Anthology.
South Brunswick, N. J. and New York: Barnes, for The
Poetry Society of America, 1971. 323 pp.
      An alphabetically arranged anthology of poems culled
from submissions by Poetry Society of America members.
The poetry is not particularly "contemporary" in spirit and
the few diamonds aren't worth the effort. Biographical notes.

ANTHOLOGY: Black Writers Workshop. Introduction by Don
L. Lee. Kansas City, Mo.: KRIZNA, 1970. 52 pp.

ATKINSON, Bob, ed. Songs of the Open Road: The Poetry
of Folk Rock & The Journey of the Hero. Foreword by
Oscar Brand. New York: Signet, NAL, 1974. 144 pp.
      Mostly song lyrics, with the work of practicing poets
like Leonard Cohen excluded. It is "a chronicle of our times"
(p. 13), "a happy excursion through contemporary folk poetry,
a new mythology born out of quadraphonic sound" (p. 14).
The collection, representing twenty authors, is divided into
three sections: songs of awakening, love, and eternity. The
two epilogues, one by the editor and one by Jung, deal with
the mythological, archetypal aspects of folk rock poetry. References to additional lyrics classic books on myth, and indexes of authors and first lines are included.

ATLAS, James, ed. Ten American Poets: An Anthology of
Poems. Cheshire, Eng.: Carcanet Press (dist. in U. S.
by Dufour), 1973. 94 pp.
      "Bias is academic ... all have been associated with
Cambridge or Harvard, and with such teachers as Lowell,
Elizabeth Bishop, and Robert Fitzgerald.... A poem's formal
qualities determine its authority" (p. 11). Alan Williamson,
Peggy Rizza, John Koethe and others are included. Notes on
the poets in the table of contents.

BECK, Dorothy, ed. Northern Lights: Writers from the Upper Valley on the Connecticut River. (Chap Book No. 1)
Hanover, N. H.: Granite Publications, 1972.
      Very uneven but nicely presented collection concen-
trating on poets from a small region--many connected with
Dartmouth. Notes on contributors.

BONAZZI, Robert, ed. Toward Winter. New Rivers/Lati-
tudes, 1972. Lithographs by Lucas Johnson.

"An anthology, including work by Bly, Wright, Merwin, Van Doren, Thomas Merton and others" (A Catalogue of Small Press Publications from Serendipity, Spring-Summer 1974).

BOWLES, Jerry G. and Russell, Tony, eds. The Book Is a Movie: An Exhibition of Language Art and Visual Poetry. New York: Dell, 1971. 320 pp. Illustrated.
        "A collection of work loosely related by the fact that all the contributors are doing something unusual with language.... Most of the work in this collection is new, much of it done specifically for the project" (p. 12). Emmett Williams, Aram Saroyan, and Armand Schwerner are among the 34 contributors experimenting with language art. Notes on poets.

BREMAN, Paul, ed. You Better Believe It: Black Verse in English from Africa, the West Indies and the United States. Middlesex, Eng.: Penguin, 1973. 552 pp.
        Two hundred selections by 125 poets arranged chronologically by date of author's birth, from George Moses Horton (1797) to Victor Hernandez Cruz (1949) and Mesu Ber (1950). "The chronological order deliberately upsets the more obvious geographical one. It is no longer useful, I think, to present the literary developments that took place in different parts of the black world as so many entirely separate streams: they are coming together, and the time has come to see the unity in their variety.... The main theme of the collection is: how have black writers, from different geographical and social backgrounds, reacted to what has become known as the 'black experience'?" (p. 19). The personalized biographies preceding each poet's work are informative, engagé, and make good reading, but the poetry selections are not always judicious. Index of authors and geographical index.

BROOKLYN Ferry: 10 New York Poets. Brooklyn, N.Y.: Brooklyn Ferry Poets Coop, 1975. 101 pp. Illustrated.
        Interesting urban poetry by Samuel Exler, Howard Ostwind, Lewis Gardner, Sally Smith, Margaret Thomson, Joan Larkin, Jay McDonnell, Virginia McGeagh, Florence Miller, Merle Molofsky. Notes on contributors.

BROOKS, Gwendolyn, ed. A Broadside Treasury. Detroit: Broadside Press, 1971. 188 pp.
        Selections from the books For Malcolm and Black Poetry, individual works of Broadside poets, and the Broadside Series. Meaty anthology. Author and title indexes.

_____. Jump Bad: A New Chicago Anthology. Detroit:
   Broadside Press, 1971. 188 pp.
      Collection of poetry and prose by young writers from
Gwendolyn Brooks' Chicago workshop. They "are blackening
English. Some of the results are effective and stirring.
Watch for them" (p. 12). The contributors include Mike
Cook, Don L. Lee, Ronda Davis and nine more. The poetry
is alive, straightforward, and a sense of excitement and com-
munity "jumps good" off the page. Brief biographies and au-
thor-title index.

BRUCHAC, Joseph and Witherup, William, eds. Words from
   the House of the Dead: Prison Writings from Soledad.
   Greenfield Center, N.Y.: Greenfield Review Press, 1971.
   67 pp. Illustrated.
      Poetry, prose, and drawings smuggled out of prison
and printed anonymously. A look at the "Inmate Manuscript
Review Form" on page 66 reveals why. The sense of frus-
tration and anger comes through.

BUKOWSKI, Charles; Cherry, Neeli; and Vangelisti, Paul.
   Anthology of L.A. Poets. Fairfax, Calif.: Red Hill
   Press, 1972.

BULKIN, Elly and Larkin, Joan, eds. Amazon Poetry: An
   Anthology of Lesbian Poetry. New York: Out & Out
   Books, 1975. 110 pp.
      Thirty-eight well known and little known poets in an
interesting collection. May Swenson, Susan Griffin, etc.
Notes on contributors.

CAPTIVE Voices: A Collection of Prose and Poetry from
   Folsom Prison. Paradise, Calif.: Dustbooks, 1975.

CARRUTH, Hayden, ed. The Voice That Is Great Within Us:
   American Poetry of the Twentieth Century. New York:
   Bantam, 1970. 722 pp.
      Representative, wide-ranging selection arranged chro-
nologically from Robert Frost to Joel Sloman, with biographical and bibliographical notes for each of the 136 poets.

CHAPMAN, Abraham, ed. Jewish-American Literature in
   Anthology. New York: Mentor/NAL, 1974. 727 pp.
      Fiction, poetry, autobiography, criticism, and a sub-
stantial introduction touching on culture, cultural imperialism

in America, and the place of the Jewish writer in the literary
mainstream.   The editor takes issue with several critical
articles on the subject of the Jewish writer in America and
concludes that Jewish-American poets, while not forming a
"school," have been influenced by the spirit of the Hebrew
literary tradition and the Jewish historical experience.   Thirty-
five poets, ranging from Bret Harte to Anita Barrows, are
represented in the 166 pages devoted to poetry.

CHESTER, Laura and Barba, Sharon, eds.   Rising Tides:
    20th Century American Women Poets.   New York: Wash-
    ington Square Press, 1973.   410 pp.   Photographs of the
    poets.
        "Most of the poems we have chosen--and we found
this kind of poem in the work of every woman we read--may
be called 'poems about women'" (p. xxvi).   The editors briefly discuss women writers and the fact that representation in
anthologies "has not gone far beyond tokenism" (p. xxiii).
Arrangement is chronological by date of birth from Gertrude
Stein to Laura Chester.   Photo and short biography of each
contributor in an enlightening, wide-ranging collection representing 70 poets.   Indexed.

CLARK, Tom, ed.   All Stars.   Santa Fe: Goliard; New York:
    Grossman, 1972.   347 pp.
        Thirteen poets representing mainly the "New York
School," including Padgett, McClure, the editor and ten
others.   In-group, playful, sometimes precious.

COLE, William, ed.   Pick Me Up: A Book of Short Short
    Poems.   New York: Macmillan, 1972.   183 pp.
        Anthology of over 200 short poems arranged themati-
cally.   Bibliographic references (catalog card).

_____.   Poems One Line & Longer.   New York: Gross-
    man, 1973.   182 pp.
        International collection of short poems arranged in a
dozen thematic sections.   It includes the work of contemporary Americans, some of which is memorable.   Lively collection.   Index of authors and first lines.

_____.   Poetry Brief: An Anthology of Short, Short Po-
    ems.   New York: Macmillan, 1971.   202 pp.
        Almost 300 poems under 13 lines from magazines
and other anthologies.   Some modern poets are represented

along with Yeats, Frost, etc. Intended as an enjoyable anthology, a gift book, but not particularly contemporary in spirit, content, or representation.

COOMBS, Orde, ed. We Speak as Liberators: Young Black
    Poets. New York: Dodd, Mead, 1970. 252 pp.
        One hundred and thirty-five poems by 57 alphabetical-
ly arranged contributors. The collection is an "assemblage
of works of infrequently published blacks who came of age--
literally and psychologically--during the horrendous American
sixties" (p. xv). Several established poets are also included,
such as Don L. Lee and Mari Evans. Good, militant collection concluding with autobiographies of the poets.

CORMAN, Cid, ed. The Gist of Origin, 1951-1971: An An-
    thology. New York: Grossman, 1975. 525 pp.
        Work published in the journal Origin, arranged by
publication date. Contributors, many from the Black Mountain Group, include Creeley, Bronk, Snyder, etc. Appendices
and notes on poets.

CURRENT Assets. Montreal: Writers' Cooperative, 1973.
    149 pp.
        Fiction and poetry, including work of seven Canadian
and American poets.

CUSTODIO, Maurice, and others, eds. Peace & Pieces: An
    Anthology of Contemporary American Poetry. Calif.:
    Peace & Pieces Foundation, 1973. 197 pp. Illus.
        "Collection of major and minor poets, many from the
San Francisco Bay Area, each represented by at least one
previously unpublished poem. Biographical notes" (Booklist,
December 15, 1975, p. 565).

DEE, Ruby, ed. Glowchild: and Other Poems. New York:
    Third Press, Odarkai Books, 1972. 111 pp.
        Mainly message poems Ruby Dee has found that teen-
ages (about 11 to 17) respond to. The selection includes over
90 poems divided into seven thematic sections written by teen-
agers, unknown and known poets, and the editor writing under
the pen-name Ann Wallace.

DODGE, Robert K. and McCullough, Joseph B., eds. Voices
    from Wah'Kon-tah: Contemporary Poetry of Native Amer-
    icans. New York: International Publishers, 1974.
    144 pp.
        In the foreword, Vine Deloria, Jr. writes, "It is a

lyrical attempt to provide a transition between the glorious
past with which we all agree and the desperate present which
Indians know and which the white man refuses to admit" (p.
12). Half of the 34 poets represented got their start at the
Institute of American Indian Arts. Notes on contributors.

DRUMMOND, Donald F., ed. A Full House of Poets. Co-
    lumbia, Mo.: Lucas Brothers, 1974. 162 pp.
    A selection of poems by 14 poets who attended the
University of Missouri at some time during the past 20 years.
An uneven collection concluding with the work of R. K. Mein-
ers and Donald Justice.

DUNCAN, William C., ed. Contemporaries: An Anthology
    of Contemporary Poetry. San Francisco: Contemporary
    Literature Press, 1975.

DUVA, Nicholas Anthony, ed. Somebody Real: Voices of
    City Children. Rockaway, N.J.: American Faculty
    Press, 1972. 184 pp. Illustrated with photos of the
    children.
        Poetry and short prose pieces by 24 Black and Puerto
Rican children from the editor's sixth grade class in a Jersey
City public school (1970-71 school year). "The words on
these pages are strong, and proud. They reflect not only the
pathos, but the warmth, and the music of being 11 or 12 and
walking, talking, living, caressing, and hating the city streets"
(p. v). A moving collection. One of Eida's poems (no last
names are given) is "LOVE": "My mother bought me/A gold
ring, /A ring that says LOVE on it. /But everybody thinks/
It's not real. "

EFROS, Susan, ed. This Is Women's Work: An Anthology
    of Prose and Poetry. San Francisco: Panjandrum Press,
    1974. 147 pp. Illustrated.
        Poetry, prose, and artwork by over 30 known and un-
known contributors, primarily from the Bay Area. Writers
include Alta, Tillie Olsen, Susan Griffin, and Marge Piercy.

ELLMANN, Richard and O'Clair, Robert, eds. The Norton
    Anthology of Modern Poetry. New York: Norton, 1973.
    1456 pp.
        Chronologically arranged collection of over 1200 po-
ems by 155 poets from Whitman to James Tate. The introduction provides an historical overview of modern poetry, and
the introductions to the selections from each poet "place them
in relation to others, as well as ... provide a sense of what

they wished their work to accomplish" (p. xiv).   Liberally
annotated, forty-page bibliography, indexes to authors, titles
and first lines.   An essential anthology--scholarly and com-
prehensive--and useful as textbook and reference tool, though
its pages are crowded and the paper thin.

ESHLEMAN, Clayton, ed.   A Caterpillar Anthology: A Selec-
    tion of Poetry and Prose from "Caterpillar" Magazine.
    Garden City, N. Y. :   Anchor Doubleday, 1971.   503 pp.
        The editor discusses the magazine and its preferences.
Selections from twelve issues follow, representing the work of
David Meltzer, Armond Schwerner and others.   Contributors'
biographies.

FERLINGHETTI, Lawrence, ed.   City Lights Anthology.   San
    Francisco: City Lights, 1974.   250 pp. Illustrated.
        Poetry, prose, mini-anthologies and manifestos--an
international collection of new writing.   Notes on contributors.

FREED, Ray, ed.   Doctor Generosity's Almanac: 17 poets.
    New York: Doctor Generosity's Press, 1970.   116 pp.
        Notes on poets.

FRIEDMAN, Hedda.   The Sound the Heart Makes: Poetry
    and Therapy.   Armonk, N. Y. :   Bale of Turtle Press,
    1972.   72 pp.   Illustrated.
        The author of most of the mediocre verse in this
volume served as a volunteer at Pilgrim State Hospital, where
she read and wrote poetry with the patients (nine of their
anonymous poems are included).   It was a laudable effort,
which the prefatory statements by professionals touch upon,
but, unfortunately, one doesn't learn much about poetry or
therapy from this book.

GATHERED from the Center: Poetry from Readings at the
    Berkeley Women's Center.   Oakland, Calif. :   Mama's
    Press, 1975.   51 pp.
        Twenty-one poets represented.

GERSMEHL, Glen, ed. and illus.   Words Among America.
    New York, 1971.   54 pp.   Illustrated.
        Sixty social and political poems plus commentary and
quotations.   Profits from the sale of the book go to the Non-
Violence Center of Chavez' United Farm Workers in San Joa-
quin Valley ($1 to 537 West 121 St. , N. Y. , N. Y.   10027).

GIBSON, Margaret and McCann, Richard, eds.   Landscape

and Distance: Contemporary Poets from Virginia. Char-
lottesville, Va.: University of Virginia Press, 1975.
89 pp.
     An uneven collection by poets who have lived in Vir-
ginia in recent years--Dabney Stuart, Henry Taylor, Anne
Winters, Annie Dillard, etc. A section of prose reflections
by the contributors on the anthology's theme.

GILDNER, Gary and Gildner, Judith, eds. Out of This World:
     Poems from the Hawkeye State. Ames, Iowa: Iowa State
     University Press, 1975. 144 pp.
          One hundred and one poems by 68 authors about Iowa,
if not by Iowans. Contributors include X. J. Kennedy, Kenneth Rosen, Nancy Price, etc.

GILL, Elaine, ed. Mountain Moving Day: Poems by Women.
     Trumansburg, N. Y.: Crossing Press, 1973. 126 pp.
     Photos of the poets.
          A small handsome anthology representing seventeen
women--five from Canada and twelve from the U. S.--put together with taste and obvious enthusiasm. Autobiographies
and photos.

GILL, John, ed. New American and Canadian Poetry. Bos-
     ten: Beacon Press, 1971. 280 pp. Photos of the poets.
          Sixteen Canadians and 18 American contemporary
poets. Lyn Lifshin, Don L. Lee, and Dick Lourie are among
the Americans representing, more or less, the poetry of "direct statement." Biographical notes.

GILLAM, C. W., ed. Eight Modern American Poets. Lon-
     don: Harrap, 1971. 150 pp.
          An introductory selection from the work of Williams,
Rexroth, Roethke, Lowell, Wilbur, Levertov, Merwin, and
Snyder. Brief outline of the history of American poetry,
commentary on the poems, and bibliography (publisher).

GIOVANNI, Nikki, ed. Night Comes Softly: Anthology of
     Black Female Voices. Newark, N. J.: Medic Press,
     1970. 97 pp.

GITLIN, Todd, ed. Campfires of the Resistance: Poetry
     from the Movement. Indianapolis, Ind.: Bobbs-Merrill,
     1971. 295 pp.
          Over 200 poems by 57 people involved in radical ac-
tivity in the 60's. "The book as a whole is about the Movement as a force and a life-activity, about an identity as well

as its enemies. It is a chronicle of radical vision in the Sixties, on the long march from issue-centered protest to total revolt against the capitalist-imperialist-racist death system" (p. xiv). The emphasis is on white, young, lesser known poets, though Jane Stembridge, Charlie Cobb, Diane di Prima, Ginsberg and other black and/or established poets are included. The arrangement for the early sixties is roughly chronological and for the later sixties alphabetical by author's name. A chronology of movement events from February 1960 to February 1970 is included. Autobiographical statements describe background, political activities, and present life style.

GREAVES, Griselda, ed.   The Burning Thorn.   New York: Macmillan, 1971.   202 pp.
    One hundred and twenty-seven poems covering a wide range of subjects, periods, and styles intended for young people with prior interest.   Indexes and notes (Library Journal, December 15, 1971, p. 4189).

GREINKE, L. Eric, ed.   Ten Michigan Poets.   Grand Rapids, Mich.: Pilot Press, 1972.   154 pp.
    Good collection of work by Cor Barendrecht, Joseph Dionne, Albert and Barbara Drake, L. Eric Greinke, John Knapp, Ronnie M. Lane, Herbert Woodward Martin, E. W. Oldenburg, and Barbara Rollins.   The poets' selections are their own.   Biobibliographical notes.

GROSS, Ronald and others, eds.   Open Poetry: Four Anthologies of Expanded Poems.   New York: Simon and Schuster, 1973.   614 pp.
    Four very different books in one: "Metapoetry: The Poetry of Changes" edited by George Quasha; "Language Happenings" edited by Emmett Williams; "Found Poetry" edited by John Robert Colombo; and "The Poetry of Survival" edited by Walter Lowenfels.   Each is prefaced by an introduction. A handsome, exciting anthology with immediate impact in the sections on concrete and Black American poetry.   Index of poems.

A GROSS of Greatness: An Anthology of Chicano Poetry with 12 Poets.   El Paso, Tex.: Barrio Publications, 1972.

HALPERN, Daniel, ed.   The American Poetry Anthology. New York: Avon, 1975.   506 pp.
    Poets and anthologist together chose works to be included.   Among the more than 70 contributors under 40: Lucille Clifton, Louise Gluck, Michael Benedikt, etc., arranged

alphabetically. Exhibits "certain tendencies that are very much of the present time: freedom of form and disengagement from political or social involvement" (The New York Times Book Review, January 4, 1976). A significant anthology opening to mixed reviews. Biographical notes.

HANNA, Charles Shahoud, ed. New American Poetry into the 80's: The Doctor Generosity Poets. Wescosville, Pa.: Damascus Road Press, 1975.
    Features poets who have read at Saturday afternoon poetry readings at Doctor Generosity's Poetry Pub (2nd Ave. and 73rd St., N.Y.C.), including poetry by and for Paul Blackburn, who originated the readings. A good collection representing the work of 66 poets. Notes on contributors.

_____. Ten Women: Their Poems. Wescosville, Pa.: Damascus Road Press, 1972. 64 pp.
    Selections by Denise Levertov, Rochelle Owens, Ruth Herschberger, Helen Adam, Marguerite Harris, Margaret Randall, Daisy Aldan, Diane Di Prima, C. G. Ogden, Carol Berge. Rochelle Owens stands out for verve. Notes on contributors.

HANNUM, Sara and Chase, John Terry, Comps. The Wind Is Round. New York: Atheneum, 1970. 100 pp. Illustrated by Ron Bowen.
    Sixty-nine nature poems by modern poets. A quiet, reflective, perhaps rather dull introduction to the established, important names of modern poetry--Howard Moss, Anne Sexton, etc. Author and title index.

HARMS, Valerie, ed. Convocation! Women in Writing. Tampa, Fla.: United Sisters, 1975. 178 pp. Illustrated.
    "A book based on the happenings of the first women writers' conference, Bridgeport, Connecticut, 1974, and an anthology of the works of the women who attended ... a cooperative effort of women, by women, for women, which represents the words of over 40 Women of Words ..." (publisher). Poems, stories, articles, etc., with autobiographical sketches of the contributors.

HARVEY, Nick, ed. Mark in Time: Portraits & Poetry/San Francisco. Photographs by Christa Fleischmann. San Francisco: Glide, 1971. 189 pp.
    "Varied faces and works of 80 poets ... belonging to or associated with the San Francisco community of poets" (p. 7). Handsome volume with wide-ranging representation includ-

ing Ginsberg, Cruz, Ishmael Reed, etc. Autobiographical
notes.

HEAD, Thomas and Foreman, Paul, eds. The San Francisco
    Bark: A Gathering of Bay Area Poets. Berkeley, Calif. :
    Thorp Springs Press, 1972.

HILL, Helen and Perkins, Agnes, comps. New Coasts and
    Strange Harbors: Discovering Poems. New York: Cro-
    well, 1974. 283 pp.
        Short, often lyrical poems which "add up to a cata-
logue of poetical devices in modern dress" (The New York
Times Book Review, December 29, 1974, p. 8). Plath, Sexton, Whittemore, and others.

HOLLYFIELD, Jeanne, ed. Dance of the Muse: A Treasure
    of Modern Poetry. Appalachia, Va. : Young, 1970.
    301 pp.
        More than 600 poems by 340 authors from the U. S.
and Canada. The poets represented are unknown and still unknown to the reader after one or two often mediocre poems.

HOPKINS, Lee Bennett, comp. City Talk. New York:
    Knopf, 1970. Photographs by Roy Arenella.
        Writing by children in the cinquain verse form, ar-
ranged thematically by season.

_____, ed. On Our Way: Poems of Pride and Love.
    New York: Knopf, 1974. 63 pp. Photos by David
    Parks.
        A handsome book--each of the 22 poems has an ap-
pealing photograph on the facing page. As for the poetry,
Adoff's My Black Me has more for the money and is a much
better selection. Indexes to titles and first lines. Notes on
the poets.

_____. Take Hold! An Anthology of Pulitzer Prize-Winning
    Poems. New York: Nelson, 1975. 96 pp.
        Poems chosen from 19 of the 53 Pulitzer prize-win-
ning volumes. "It seems designed to prove what many ob-
servers have long held: that over its long history, the Pulitzer committee has been timid, narrow, conventional, gutless
and perhaps uninformed" (The New York Times Book Review,
December 29, 1974, p. 8).

_____, and Rasch, Sunna, eds. I Really Want to Feel
    Good About Myself! Poems by Former Drug Addicts.

New York: Nelson, 1974.
"The statements that precede these poems ... are
more revealing than the formal efforts that follow" (The New
York Times Book Review, December 29, 1974, p. 8).

HOUGH, Henry W. , ed. Golden Harvest: The Poetry Society
of Colorado, 1921-1971. Boulder, Col. : Pruett, 1971.
245 pp.

HOWARD, Richard. Preferences: 51 American Poets Choose
Poems from Their Own Work & from the Past. Photographs by Thomas Victor. New York: Viking, 1974.
323 pp.
        Lavishly produced anthology of preferences--poems
from the present and the past (pre-1900) which, "in some
sense, fit"--and full-page black and white photos of the contributors as well as erudite explication and commentary on
the poets' choices, techniques, etc. The editor/poet/critic
would like to see contemporary poetry help us read, under-
stand and transform the poetry of the past--past and present
shedding light on each other. This anthology of white, established, mostly well known poets contrasts with and supple-
ments Rothenberg and Quasha's America A Prophecy (N. Y. :
Random, 1973) which also looks back but from an entirely
different perspective and temperament. In alphabetical order
the contributors range from A. R. Ammons to James Wright.
The preferences include Donald Finkel's "The Cross-Eyed
Lover" and his choice--Keats "La Belle Dame Sans Merci";
Anne Sexton's "In the Deep Museum" and her choice--Rilke's
"Christ's Descent into Hell"; and Robert Penn Warren's
"Mortmain" alongside Henry Vaughan's "Corruption. " Three-
syllable words of explication are preferred to one and the
price and bias toward the academic and contemplative limit
popular accessibility.

HOWE, Florence, and Bass, Ellen, eds. No More Masks!
An Anthology of Poems by Women. Garden City, N. Y. :
Anchor Doubleday, 1973. 396 pp.
        A chronological arrangement of the work of 87 poets
of the twentieth century reflecting a multiplicity of themes,
feelings, forms, and ideas. An excellent collection of established and less well known poets. Includes biographical notes.

HSIN-FU WAND, David, ed. Asian-American Heritage: An
Anthology of Prose and Poetry. New York: Washington
Square Press, 1974. 308 pp. Illustrated with photos.
        An anthology of stories, essays, novel excerpts, and

oral poetry (Hawaiian and Samoan chants) which includes 42
poems by thirteen poets, most of them contemporary. A
small, varied sampling. Janice Mirikitani stands out. Introductions, biographical sketches, glossary, and bibliography
of suggested further reading.

THE IMMANENTIST Anthology: Art of the Superconscious.
New York: The Smith, 1973. 120 pp. Illustrated.
       Nineteen poets representing a movement founded by
Duane Locke, who is a contributor to the volume and writes
the philosophical introduction. Imagistic, sometimes surreal-
istic work. Notes on poets accompany the selections.

IVERSON, Lucille and Ruby, Kathryn, eds. We Become New:
Poems by Contemporary American Women. New York:
Bantam, 1975. 234 pp.
       Forty-three known and unknown contributors and an
introduction which describes "feminist poetry, like black
verse," as "a poetry of change, a populist poetry" (p. xii)
and discusses the need for a separate collection of women's
work. The volume suggests the "major concerns and chang-
ing perspectives of American women" (p. xiii). Notes on
contributors.

JAMES, Nancy Esther and Balazs, Mary Webber, eds. I,
That Am Ever Stranger: Poems on Woman's Experience.
Faculty Research Fund of Westminster College, New
Wilmington, Pa. and American Association of University
Women Educational Foundation, 1974. 68 pp.
       Ninety-three poems by 73 known and unknown poets
expressing a range of attitudes, viewpoints, and experiences.
"Following the poems on woman's traditional roles are poems
'in search of viable alternatives.' ... Some of the alternatives
presented here are extramarital affairs, separation and di-
vorce, life without men or children, prostitution, madness,
and religion. This section concludes with poems presenting
woman as artist. A final group portrays older women and
widows" (preface). Notes on contributors.

JORDAN, June, ed. Soulscript: Afro-American Poetry.
Garden City, N.Y.: Zenith Books, Doubleday, 1970.
144 pp.
       "Poems are voiceprints of language, or if you prefer,
soulscript" (pp. xvi-xvii). Seven thematically labeled sections
prefaced by a short introductory prose/poem. The first section showcases the work of nine poets aged 12-18 (mediocre).
The other sections include selections by older well known

poets and contemporary figures such as Nikki Giovanni and
Julius Lester. Not the best of the Black anthologies. Notes
on contributors. Indexes of first lines and authors.

_____. and Bush, Terri, eds. The Voice of the Chil-
     dren. New York: Holt, Rinehart and Winston, 1970.
     101 pp. Illustrated with photos of the poets.
          Poetry and prose by 26 Black and Puerto Rican chil-
     dren, ages 9 to 15, who participated in a creative writing
     workshop in the Fort Greene section of Brooklyn conducted by
     the editors. Several memorable and poignant pieces. Indexes
     of titles and authors.

KAMINISKI, Margaret, ed. Moving to Antarctica: An Anthol-
     ogy of Women's Writing. (American Dust Series, No. 2)
     Paradise, Calif.: Dustbooks, 1975. 163 pp.
          Prose and poetry from Moving Out (Vol. 1, no. 1,
     March 1971 to Vol. 5, no. 2, Fall 1975) by known and un-
     known writers--Robin Morgan, Alta, etc. Biographical notes.

KENNEDY, Dick and others. The Yes! Press Anthology.
     Santa Barbara, Calif.: Christopher's Books, 1972.
     53 pp.
          "An anthology of the Yes! Press Broadsheet series
     plus a few previously unpublished poems by Diana Di Prima,
     Lew Welch, David Meltzer, Gary Snyder, Jack Hirshman,
     and others. Bibliography of the broadsheets. Biographical
     notes" (Booklist, December 15, 1975, p. 567).

KHERDIAN, David, ed. Settling America: The Ethnic Ex-
     pression of 14 Contemporary Poets. New York: Mac-
     millan, 1974. 126 pp.
          A poetic exploration of roots, identities, and assimi-
     lation with biographies and personal statements by the poets,
     including Corso, Cruz, and others. A fascinating idea and
     good collection.

_____. Visions of America by the Poets of Our Time.
     New York: Macmillan, 1973. 92 pp. Illustrated by
     Nonny Hogrogian.
          About 60 poems reflecting the heritage of W. C.
     Williams and the language of speech, divided into three sec-
     tions: growing up, in America, and its cities. Biographical
     notes and indexes to authors, titles, and first lines.

_____. and Baloian, James, eds. Down at the Santa Fe
     Depot: 20 Fresno Poets. Fresno, Calif.: Giligia Press,

1970.   143 pp.   Illustrated with photos.
Handsome anthology of generally high caliber work.
The poets are arranged alphabetically.   Robert Mezey, Dennis
Saleh, and Luis Omar Salinas are among the contributors.
Photos and autobiographies.

KING, Woodie, ed.   BlackSpirits: A Festival of New Black
    Poets in America.   New York: Random, 1972.   253 pp.
        Don L. Lee writes the introduction--an introduction
to Black poetry and the cultural scene.   The anthology represents the work of 30 contemporary Black poets emanating from
a poetry production produced by Woodie King Associates.
Biographical notes.

KLONSKY, Milton.   Shake the Kaleidoscope: A New Anthol-
    ogy of Modern Poetry.   New York: Pocket Books, 1973.
    332 pp.   (Second printing in 1975 with new title, The Best
    of Modern Poetry.)
        Over 100 English and American poets and 300 poems
for "an overall view of the constantly shifting and multifaceted
varieties of modern poetry" (p. xxx).   The editor chose the
less publicized and personally authentic rather than historically significant poems (providing a sampling rather than depth)
and omitted many better known modern poets.   "Poets with
an affinity through style or temperament have been grouped
together" (pp. xxx-xxxi).   A surprising and wide-ranging
anthology.   The original title fits.   Notes on the poets and
index of first lines.

_____.   Speaking Pictures.   A Gallery of Pictorial Poetry
    from the Sixteenth Century to the Present.   New York:
    Harmony/Crown, 1975.   333 pp.   Illustrated.
        The substantial introduction provides a historical over-
view of visual or pictorial poetry, and contemporary Americans are well represented, including Jane Augustine, Carol
Bankerd, and May Swenson.   Biographical notes combined
with author index.   Bibliography.

KOHL, Herbert and Cruz, Victor Hernandez.   Stuff: A Col-
    lection of Poems, Visions & Imaginative Happenings from
    Young Writers in Schools--Open & Closed.   New York:
    World, 1970.   122 pp.   Illustrated.
        Includes oral poetry, poetry passed on to the editors
by teachers, poetry from over 3,000 pages of material.
Notes on the 49 contributors, ranging in age from five years
to 20+.

KONGLOMERATI.   Gulfport, Fla.: Konglomerati Press,

1972. Illustrated.
A hip, lively collection representing 25 poets including Kostelanetz, Malanga, Waldman, etc.

KOSTELANETZ, Richard, ed. Imaged Words & Worded Images. New York: Outerbridge and Dienstfrey, 1970.
101 pp.
The editor discusses the incorporation of word within image and the background and significance of "word-imagery. " "'Typographical devices, employed with great daring, '
wrote Apollinaire, 'have given rise to a visual lyricism al-
most unknown before our time, ' and in the best word-imagery
are both profound perceptual experiences and unprecedented
forms of art-and-communication which in sum realize the
classic ideal of the possible fusion, within one inclusive form,
of both poetry and painting. The following selection, most of
which has not appeared in books before, intends to represent
examples of the best word-imagery.... All the practitioners
included here are living and working today" (n. p.). Ninety-
six word images by a varied group, including Americans John
Hollander, Emmett Williams, Robert Indiana, etc. Coffee
table poetry/art, handsome and fun, even if sometimes Mad
Ave. gimmicky. Biographical notes.

_____. Possibilities of Poetry: An Anthology of American
Contemporaries. New York: Dell, Delta, 1970. 526 pp.
Forty-four post-World War II poets with each individual's poems appearing in order of publication. The editor's
introduction is an interesting survey of the modern scene.
Biobibliographies, index of authors and titles, and index of
first lines.

LANE, Ronnie M. , ed. Face the Whirlwind. Grand Rapids,
Mich. : Pilot Press, 1973. 95 pp.
"Ten of Michigan's best Black poets"--Stella Crews,
Robert Hayden, Naomi Long Madgett, Herbert Woodward Mar-
tin, Dudley Randall, James Randall, Jon Randall, Richard
Thomas, June D. Whaley, and Jill Witherspoon-Boyer--select-
ing from their own work. Notes on poets.

LARRICK, Nancy, ed. I Heard a Scream in the Street: Poems by Young People in the City. New York: Evans,
1970. 141 pp. Illustrated with photos from the Annual
Scholastic Magazine/Eastman Kodak Contest.
Seventy-seven poems selected from over 5000 city
poems by young people (ages 9 to 18) in 23 American cities.
Many were chosen from school newspapers and the under-

ground student press. A handsome volume divided into five
thematic sections. Index of poets and titles. Index of first
lines.

_____ . Room for Me and a Mountain Lion: Poetry of Open
Space. New York: Evans, 1974. 191 pp. Illustrated
with photographs.
   One hundred and two, mostly contemporary, nature
poems "selected with the help of young readers who revel in
what Whitman calls, 'eating and sleeping with the earth'" (p.
13). Index of poems and poets and index of first lines.

LARSON, Clinton and Stafford, William, eds. Modern Poetry
   of Western America. Provo, Utah: Brigham Young University Press, 1975.

LASK, Thomas, ed. The New York Times Book of Verse.
   (A New York Times book) New York: Macmillan, 1970.
   552 pp.
   Poetry from the editorial pages of The New York
Times published over the past 50 years. The poetry covers
a wide range of topics and represents the work of known and
unknown poets. Contemporary in tone but not avant-garde or
inaccessible; the aim "is simply to provide a body of work
that will be a pleasure to read," salvaged "from the transitory
nature of newspaper publications" (p. xiii). Author and title
indexes.

LEE, Al, ed. The Major Young Poets. New York: World,
   1971. 200 pp.
   The eight poets represented (Michael Benedikt, James
Tate, Mark Strand, Wm. Brown, David P. Young, C. K. Williams, Charles Simic, Marvin Bell) are arranged alphabetically. Inclusion was based on two criteria: "'Major' means
quantity as well as quality.... 'Young' I have applied to poets no older than 35 as of January 1, 1970" (p. 4). The editor describes the diversity, explicitness, and absence of
theory in the contemporary "esthetic." A hip collection of
high caliber, but the title is misleading--A Few Major Young
Male Poets would be more accurate. Biographies, bibliographies, and indexes of titles and first lines are included.

LESBIANS Speak Out. Calif.: Women's Press Collective,
   1974. 154 pp. Illus.
   "An expanded, graphically enriched edition of a mim-
eographed item distributed at a West Coast conference. Prose
and poetry by 80 lesbians display the emotions and politics of

the early stages of the gay women's liberation movement.
Brief bibliography" (Booklist, December 15, 1975, p. 563).

LEYLAND, Winston, ed.   Angels of the Lyre: A Gay Poetry
    Anthology.   San Francisco: Panjandrum/Gay Sunshine,
    1975.   248 pp.   Illustrated.
        Well reviewed anthology of 57 American and Canadian
poets selected by the editor of Gay Sunshine.   All of the work
was written in the last 25 years--most in the last ten--and
most had appeared in Gay Sunshine.   The introduction offers
a bibliographical and historical review of gay poetry.   Contributors, including Malanga, Goodman, Spicer, etc., are arranged alphabetically.   Biographical notes.

LOMAX, Alan and Abdul, Raoul, eds.   3000 Years of Black
    Poetry: An Anthology.   New York: Dodd, Mead, 1970.
    261 pp.
        Poets born after 1920 are represented in the section
"Black American Poets" and include Mari Evans, Julian Bond,
Nikki Giovanni, and ten more, with one or two poems and a
brief biographical note for each.   Not the book with which
to explore contemporary black poetry.   It presents a broad
chronological and geographical view, from ancient Africa
and Egypt to Modern Africa and the U.S.A.   The aim
is range rather than depth, and in the last section, the emphasis is on hard-hitting social poems, many anthologized before and after this book.   A brief introduction precedes each
geographical section and relates music, poetry, and social
context.

LOUIS, Louise, ed.   Peopled Parables: An Anthology of
    Verse.   Westwood, N.J.: Pen-Art, 1975. 100 pp.
    Illustrated.
        "Based on the Will Anthony Madden Human Interest
award in the Fifth Annual Awards Contest of the New York
Poetry Forum, Inc."

LOURIE, Dick, ed.   Come to Power: Eleven Contemporary
    American Indian Poets.   (Crossing Press Series of Con-
    temporary Anthologies)   Trumansburg, N.Y.: Crossing
    Press, 1974.   127 pp.
        Fine, handsome anthology including Suzan Shown, Win-
ston Mason, Duane Niatum and others, with an introduction
by Joseph Bruchac, also a contributor.   Biographical notes.

LOWENFELS, Walter, ed.   From the Belly of the Shark: A
    New Anthology of Native Americans.   New York: Vintage,
    1973.   353 pp.

"Unique in that it brings together for the first time
representative poems by descendants of the original inhabitants
of our country" (p. xxv), who have been largely ignored by
"the white literary junta." The editor says that the crime of
this junta is to deny "cultural validity to over thirty millions
living in the United States" (p. xxvi), resulting in deprivation
for white and cultural genocide for non-white. About 200 selections are arranged alphabetically by writer's name within
the following sections: Indian, Chicano, Eskimo, Hawaiian,
Puerto Rican, "Traditional Indian Poems," "Related Poems
by white and Black Americans." Each section is preceded
by a signed, engagé introduction. Fine anthology, well worth
reading. Brief notes on contributors.

LUDEN, C. K., ed. Across U.S.A.: An Anthology of Po-
    etry. Sioux Falls, S.D.: Manitou Publishing Co., 1974.
    91 pp.

LUTES, Linda, ed. and artist. 7 Poets 7 Poems. Provi-
    dence, R.I.: Burning Deck Press, 1974. 7 pp. Illus-
    trated.
        Portfolio of poems by Benedikt, Bronk, Harper,
Honig, Owens, Wakoski, and Waldrop, with accompanying silk-
screened portraits. The edition is limited to 75 and the cost
is $50.00.

McCULLOUGH, Francis Monson, ed. Earth, Air, Fire, Wa-
    ter: A Collection of Over 125 Poems. New York: Co-
    ward, McCann & Geoghegan, 1971. 190 pp.
        Poems "chosen because of what might be called their
specific gravity: the pull they exert on their readers" (p. 17).
Most of the poets are contemporary Americans writing on poetry and modern life in a compilation aimed at teenage readers (and older). Some of the younger poets include Tom
Clark, Clark Coolidge, Victor Hernandez Cruz, Al Young, etc.
A mixed bag. Author and title index and notes on the poets.

McGOVERN, Ann, ed. Voices from Within: The Poetry of
    Women in Prison. Weston, Conn.: Magic Circle Press,
    1975. 32 pp.
        Writer Ann McGovern used Kenneth Koch-like techni-
ques with long-termers at the Bedford Hills Correctional Facility, New York State's only prison for women. The selections are by seven contributors, and the proceeds go to the
women. Introduction (publisher).

McGOVERN, Robert and Snyder, Richard, eds. Our Only

Hope Is Humor: Some Public Poems. Ashland, Ohio:
Ashland Poetry Press, 1972.
      "Serious funny poems" by Nemerov, Bruchac, Kuzma,
Ignatow, Lifshin, and others (publisher).

_____.   _____. 60 on the 60's: A Decade's History in
Verse. Ashland, Ohio: Ashland Poetry Press, 1970.
      "Sixty-two public and germane poems by Auden,
Brooks, Kennedy, Lowell, Snodgrass, Wilbur, and thirty-seven
others.... Widely adopted as a 'relevant' textbook (publisher).
Foreword by Senator Eugene J. McCarthy.

McMAHON, Michael, ed. Flowering After Frost: The Antho-
      logy of Contemporary New England Poetry. Boston:
      Branden Press, 1975. 120 pp.
      A good collection representing 22 well known and les-
ser known poets including Allan Block, Lyn Lifshin, John Stevens Wade, and D. W. Donzella.

MALLEY, Jean and Tokay, Halé, eds. Contemporaries:
      Twenty-eight New American Poets. New York: Viking,
      1972. 227 pp.
      Poetry "by young poets, most of whom are in their
twenties. Half of the poets are women." Includes brief notes
on the poets. Alta, John Thomas, and the editors are among
the contributors writing on current concerns in a variety of
styles. An uneven, hip, flavor-pack poetry grab bag.

MALLORY, Lee, ed. Twenty Times in the Same Place: An
      Anthology of Santa Barbara Poetry. Goleta, Calif. :
      Painted Cave Books, 1973. 168 pp. Illustrated.
      Kenneth Rexroth introduces this collection of over 100
poems by 20 poets, mainly in their mid-thirties and coming
from the Santa Barbara area (Choice, December 1974, p.
1478). Biographical notes.

MATILLA, Alfredo and Silén, Iván, eds. The Puerto Rican
      Poets/Los Poetas Puertorriqueños. New York: Bantam,
      1972. 238 pp.
      "The purpose of this anthology is to bring together
most of the important Puerto Rican poetry of this century for
both Spanish--and English--speaking readers.... It is also
the first volume to include poems that express the full range
of the Puerto Rican's experience in New York" (p. xiii). The
book is divided into three parts: "Most Important Poets before 1955," "The Major Poets," and "Latest Poetry (from
1955)." The prologue provides a brief introduction to twen-

tieth century Puerto Rican poetry, which is viewed as, with
a few exceptions, "a struggle against the agony of the ghetto
(in the colony and the metropolis) and against the imposition
of a crushing colonial state of mind" (p. xviii). The third
section consists of 38 poems by 16 writers selected as the
most representative of the younger poets, though one group,
according to the editors, did not wish to cooperate on the
anthology. The selections are arranged chronologically by
date of author's birth. The translation from English or Spanish is on the facing page. Bibliographies for the contributors
are included.

MILLER, Adam David, ed. <u>Dices or Black Bones: Black</u>
    <u>Voices of the 70's.</u> Boston: Houghton Mifflin, 1970.
    142 pp. Illustrated.
        Seventeen poets "writing out of an Afro experience."
Notes on the poets.

MINES, Stephanie and Rogoff, Alice, eds. <u>Noe Valley Poets</u>
    <u>Workshop Anthology.</u> Noe Valley Poets.
        "Although a range of poets is presented ... the tone
is mellow" (<u>Book People Small Press Checklist</u>, 1975).

MODINE Gunch Anthology. Madison, Wis.: Wisconsin Union
    Literary Committee, 1972. Illustrated.
        "Brings together poems written by poets sponsored to
read in Madison by the Union Literary Committee." Twenty-
two poets are represented.

MOLLENKOTT, Virginia, ed. <u>Adam Among the Television</u>
    <u>Trees: An Anthology of Verse by Contemporary Chris-</u>
    <u>tian Poets.</u> Waco, Tex.: Word Books, 1971. 215 pp.
        Two hundred and one poems by 41 American poets
ranging widely in age, occupation, poetic technique, etc. The
editor's aim is to demonstrate that "Christ is still a dynamic
aesthetic impetus" (p. 9) and "to put into the hands of people
in general, but especially of the Christian churchgoer, a collection of poetry which is real and honest and artistically
serious (and therefore disturbing) as opposed to the reassuring
pablum which many have all their lives regarded as poetry"
(p. 10). Cliché versifiers and readily accessible widely rec-
ognized Christian poets were omitted; the volume is "a mi-
crocosm of serious Christian poetry ... not all the artistry
is of equal quality. Some poems are relatively weak, provided for purposes of contrast ... arranged for maximum
variety ..." (pp. 13-14). The selections are preceded by a
biography and a statement of the poet's artistic/religious

credo. The selections are uneven, often provocative, sometimes memorable, but, by including weaker work, the editor
violates one of the book's aims and leaves open the question
raised by one contributor: "Are we riding Christ's coattails
into print?" Poets include Elisavietta Ritchie, Roderick Har-
tigh Jellema, and Elmer F. Suderman. Topical and thematic
index. Index of authors and titles. Index of first lines (in-
correctly labeled).

MOLLOY, Paul, ed. Beach Glass: And Other Poems. New
    York: Four Winds Press, 1970. 205 pp.
        Poems by Whitman, Frost, Ferlinghetti, and many
others "that ring with the American idiom in all its unre-
hearsed natural rhythm and colloquial swiftness" (p. 1). An ample,
representative selection. Indexed.

        . One Hundred Plus American Poems. New York:
    Scholastic Book Services, 1970. 208 pp. Illustrated with
    photographs selected from the Scholastic-Kodak Photo-
    graphy Awards, 1964-1969.
        An introductory anthology designed for young people,
with the more difficult poems at the end of each of the seven
thematic sections. Classics as well as modern works representing, among others, Langston Hughes, Robert Bly and May
Swenson. Notes on terms and references at the back and an
index of poems and poets.

MOORE, Lilian and Thurman, Judith, comps. To See the
    World Afresh. New York: Atheneum, 1974. 120 pp.
        "An anthology of readable, thought-provoking poems
by modern poets for young people of the seventies" (publisher).

MORSE, David. Grandfather Rock. New York: Dell, 1972.
    188 pp.
        A collection, with commentaries and references to
recordings of poetry and lyrics, of rock lyrics and traditional
poems spanning 3,000 years. The book is divided into seven
thematic sections in which the poems "speak to each other."
For example, "Albatross" by Judy Collins is juxtaposed with
Amy Lowell's "Patterns." Intended for teenagers--possibly as
a supplementary text. Brief bibliography. Index of titles,
authors and performers and index of first lines.

MURPHY, Beatrice M., ed. Today's Negro Voices: Anthol-
    ogy by Young Negro Poets. New York: Messner, 1970.
    141 pp.
        A nice collection of work by 33 poets under 30 (ar-

ranged alphabetically), intended for young readers, to whom
the dated packaging and the editor's over-30, well-meaning
poems will probably not appeal.

NIATUM, Duane, ed. Carriers of the Dream Wheel: Con-
     temporary Native American Poetry. New York: Harper
     & Row, 1975. 300 pp. Illustrated.
          Sixteen poets including Wendy Rose, James Welch,
N. Scott Momaday and others represented by an ample selection of reflective, personal poems. Glossary, biographical
notes, and photos of the poets.

NICHOLAS, A. X., ed. The Poetry of Soul. New York:
     Bantam, 1971. 103 pp. Illustrated.
          A collection of lyrics which is divided into four parts:
passion, pain, protest, and celebration, as sung by Nina Si-
mone, Aretha Franklin, Otis Redding, Curtis Mayfield, Ray
Charles, Issac Hayes, and others (publisher). Discography.

OCHESTER, Ed, ed. Natives: An Anthology of Contempo-
     rary American Poetry. Madison, Wis.: Quixote Press,
     n.d. Illustrated with photos.
          "Not one of the poets here is writing about anything
other than the quality of American life at the present time ...
the roots of that life, and who screws whom and why." The
known and unknown poets include Tom Clark and Erica Jong,
and the collection is strong, direct, and sometimes mockingly
funny.

ORTEGO, Philip D., ed. We Are Chicanos: An Anthology
     of Mexican-American Literature. New York: Washing-
     ton Square Press, 1973. 330 pp. Illustrated with photos
     and drawings.
          The preface provides background information on Chi-
canos, the second largest minority in the U.S. and largest
linguistic group. The anthology offers "a well-balanced selection from modern and contemporary Mexican-American
writers whose literary attitudes bear importantly on contemporary Chicano writers" (p. xv). The scope "is both thematic and generic rather than historical or chronological" (p.
xvi). Young writers are represented and an effort was made
to balance the representation of men and women. The book
is designed as a text and/or an introduction to a neglected
body of American literature. The two parts are subdivided
into sections with short commentaries. Seventy-three pages
are devoted to poetry--35 poems by 20 poets--including the
work of Luis Omar Salinas and Ricardo Sánchez. The poetry

is socially conscious but the selection is uneven and on the
whole a disappointment. Glossary and list of suggested further readings.

OWEN, Guy and Williams, Mary C. , eds. New Southern Po-
    ets: Selected Poems from "Southern Poetry Review. "
    Chapel Hill: University of North Carolina Press, 1974.
    132 pp.
        "A collection of carefully selected poems from the
entire fifteen-year span of Southern Poetry Review. " Among
the seventy poets included are James Dickey, A. R. Ammons,
Donald Justice, Heather Miller, etc. (publisher).

PADGETT, Ron and Shapiro, David, eds. An Anthology of
    New York Poets. New York: Vintage, 1970. 588 pp.
    Illustrated with drawings by Joe Brainard.
        Includes the work of 27 poets for whom New York
City is a kind of home base and who have been an influence
on each other and other poets. The contributors selected and
arranged their own work for the volume and include Frank
Lima, Frank O'Hara, Aram Saroyan, Tom Clark, etc. The
"Biographies and Bibliographies" are accompanied by a small
photo of the poet (John Giorno's biography is not to be taken
seriously in his reincarnation as Elvis Presley!). Index of
first lines.

PATTERSON, Lindsay, ed. A Rock Against the Wind: Black
    Love Poems. New York: Dodd, Mead, 1973. 172 pp.
        Ten sections--"The Joys of Love," "Love Is Hell, "
etc. --by Sonia Sanchez, Mari Evans, and others.

PECK, Richard, ed. Mindscapes: Poems for the Real World.
    New York: Dell/Delacorte, 1971. 169 pp.
        Eleven thematic sections "designed to emphasize com-
munication through a collection of poems, mostly modern, that
deal in encounters with a real, hectic, unpretty, and recog-
nizable world" (introduction). Straightforward, especially appealing to a young audience (there are even a couple of shark
poems!). Indexes of first lines, authors, titles.

        . Sounds and Silences: Poetry for Now. New York:
    Dell/Delacorte, 1970. 178 pp.
        Over 100 poems in 12 thematic sections (love, pain,
childhood, etc.), mainly written by modern American poets,
including songwriters Pete Seeger, Woody Guthrie, etc. Indexes of first lines, authors, titles.

QUASHA, George and Fremont, Susan, eds. An Active An-
    thology. Michigan: Sumac, 1974. 256 pp. Illustrated.
        Poems, many long, gathered from 64 poets with
whom the editors have personal contact (except for Charles
Olson)--Padgett, Oppenheimer, MacLow, Waldman, etc. "Inclusive" selection.

QUIST, Susan, ed.   The Cherry Valley Anthology. New York:
    Cherry Valley Anthology, 1975. 44 pp.
        Small typed anthology of well known and lesser known
poets, mainly a New York crowd.

RANDALL, Dudley, ed.   The Black Poets. New York: Ban-
    tam, 1971. 353 pp.
        In the introduction, the editor reviews other Black
anthologies and defends this one as providing a "full range of
black American poetry, from the slave songs to the present
day" (p. xxiv). It reaches for depth, includes poets not yet
anthologized, and records the progress of Black poets from
the emulation of white models to the creation of a new poetry.
The shorter first part includes Folk Poetry; the second part,
Literary Poetry, is divided into chronological sections.   List-
ings of publishers of Black poetry, periodicals publishing
Black poetry, records, tapes, video tapes, and films are provided.

ROSEN, Kenneth, ed.   Voices of the Rainbow: Contemporary
    Poetry by American Indians. New York: Viking, 1975.
    232 pp. Illustrated.
        Among others, includes "a large selection of excel-
lent poems by Leslie Silko ... one of the best writers of her
generation" (Choice, November 1975, p. 1171).

ROSENBLUM, Martin J., ed.   Brewing: 20 Milwaukee Poets.
    Giligia, 1972. 143 (or 4) pp. Illustrated. With photo-
graphs by G. Reed.
        Includes the work of Dawn Knight, Geoff Gajewski,
Tom Montag, Bob Watt, Celia Young, etc. (publisher).

ROTHENBERG, Jerome and Quasha, George, eds. America
    A Prophecy: A New Reading of American Poetry from
    Pre-Columbian Times to the Present. New York: Ran-
    dom, 1973. 603 pp.
        Collection of North American poetry including mater-
ial that would not have been regarded as poetry a few years
ago. Folklore, native song, ritual, etc., seen through the
eyes of "the continuous present," and contemporary experi-

mental work is arranged thematically in "non-chronological juxtaposition, suggestive of what T. S. Eliot called the 'simultaneous existence' and 'simultaneous order' of all poetries of all times" (p. xxiii). Sections--"Maps" and "Books"--plot stages "in the evolution of consciousness" and the "ways in which poetic functions have been handled in America" (p. xxxiv). Quotations and commentary weave through the text. Many well-known poets were excluded and non-native poets included. "Our general intention has been to show modes of poetry rather than individual poets ... the important revival of the long poem and poetic sequence in American poetry" (p. xxxvi). The introduction concludes with "A Note on Kindred Publications" including a listing of active smaller poetry presses. The introduction is in itself an essay in poetics, and the poetry, while not always contemporary, has been selected by the poet/editors from the viewpoint of a contemporary consciousness. Index, mainly of authors with dates.

ROTTMANN, Larry; Barry, Jan; and Paquet, Basil T. , eds.
Winning Hearts & Minds: War Poems by Vietnam Vets.
New York: McGraw-Hill, 1972. 116 pp. Illustrated.
        "The poetry is arranged as a series of shifting scenes which describe, in rough chronological order, a tour of combat duty in S. E. Asia. The poems, which span a period of the last ten years, also chronicle the GI's growing emotional and moral involvement with the people and the land. Thirty-three poets, contributing from one to a dozen poems each, give W. H. A. M. a diversity of voices, experiences and talents. Some of the contributors have been previously published; most have not" (p. v). An anthology which is also a document of historical and moral significance. Index of authors and their military affiliation. Several suggestions for reading, sharing, and using poetry conclude the book.

RUDGE, Mary R. , ed. Poets in Oakland. Oakland, Calif. :
Front Row Experience, 1975.
        Thirty contributors, some calligraphic work, and guest poet, Rod McKuen. Notes on editorial staff.

SCHAEFER, Charles E. and Mellor, Kathleen C. , eds.
Young Voices. New York: Bruce, 1971. 148 pp.
        One hundred and twenty-three poems in six thematic sections selected from 21,000 poems by fourth, fifth, and sixth graders in the New York Metropolitan area. The project was sponsored by the Creativity Center of Fordham University. Grade and school identification are given under each poet's name.

SCHUCK, Majorie, ed. <u>Poetry Ventured: A Poetry Anthology.</u>
    St. Petersburg, Fla. : Poetry Venture Publications, 1972.
    154 pp.
        "A collection of poems from the eight previously pub-
lished issues of Poetry Venture, Vol. 1, No. 1 through Vol.
4, No. 2, 1968-1972. " Nearly 200 poems by 145 little known
poets, over one-third from Florida. An uneven collection.
Index of authors.

SEGNITZ, Barbara and Rainey, Carol, eds. <u>Psyche: The</u>
    <u>Feminine Poetic Consciousness: An Anthology of Modern</u>
    <u>American Women Poets.</u> New York: Dial, 1973. 256 pp.
        Over 100 selections by 20 poets preceded by a criti-
cal introduction touching on psychology and women's poetry
and the place of individual poets vis-à-vis the emotional, confessional mode and the cooler intellectual, less autobiographical tendency. The anthology "concentrates on ten women
whom we consider to be major poets, i. e. , good, serious,
and original: Emily Dickinson, Elinor Wylie, Marianne
Moore, Gwendolyn Brooks, May Swenson, Denise Levertov,
Anne Sexton, Adrienne Rich, Sylvia Plath, and Margaret At-
wood. ... we have included a briefer introduction to many
newer or younger poets who suggest provocative directions"
(p. 16). The criterion for inclusion of specific poems was
quality, though they do provide insights into the condition of
women and women poets. A good collection. The introduction has pretensions to being better than it is, but the poems
are fine. Brief biographies.

SEIDMAN, Hugh and Whyatt, Francis, eds. <u>Equal Time.</u>
    New York: Equal Time Press, 1972. 101 pp.
        Good representative modern collection in an oversized
paperback. Sixty-eight contributors.

<u>SEVEN Poets at Bank Street.</u> New York: 7 Poets Press,
    1975. Illustrated with photos of the poets.
        Thomas Di Grazia, Lily Hoffman, Sharon Olds,
Jeanne Dixon, Nina Williams Leichter, Victoria Sullivan, and
George Troutt, "parents of children at Bank Street School,
first read these poems at a poetry evening to benefit the
school. " Notes.

<u>A SHINING Pane of Glass.</u> New York City, 1975. 27 pp.
        "This is a selection of the poetry written in the work-
shop directed by Brian Swann at the YM-YWHA, 92nd. St. ,
New York City, from October 1974 to January 1975. " One
example of the many small, fleeting anthologies coming out

of workshops and institutions, funded cooperatively or with government support.

SHIRINIAN, Lorne, ed. Armenian-North American Poets: An Anthology. Quebec: Manna Publishing, 1974. 104 pp. Photos of the poets.
     Twenty-one contributors from the U. S. and Canada, including Archie Minasian, Diana Der Hovanessian, and David Kherdian. Biobibliographies.

SIMMONS, Ted, comp. The Venice Poetry Company Presents ... Poems from the Venice/Calif./Coffeehouse Readings & More/More. Beverly Hills, Calif.: Venice Poetry Co., 1972. 52 pp.

SIX Poets. Ellensburg, Wash.: Vagabond Press, 1973. 71 pp. Illustrated.
     A good collection of work by Al Masarik, Lyn Lifshin, John Thomas, Ronald Koertge, Joes Deutsch, and Ann Menebroker. A homemade looking production with drawings of the poets by Charles Bukowski.

The SMITH Poets. New York: The Smith, 1971. 262 pp.
     Seven poets--Gene Fowler, Sam Cornish, Irene Schram, Theodore Sloane, Charles Wyatt, Karen Swenson, and Jonathan Morse--combined seven books into one volume. Biographical notes.

The SMITH/17: 11 Young Poets. New York: The Smith, 1975. 176 pp.
     Selections of poems by Berry, Costley, Livingston, James Ryan Morris, Richard Morris, Philbrick, Potts, Porter, Rios, Jared Smith, and Townley, each with its own title and introduction. A general introduction by editor Harry Smith (publisher).

SORRELLS, Rosalie, ed. What, Woman, and Who, Myself, I Am. Sonoma, Calif.: Wooden Shoe Press, 1974. 84pp.
     "Anthology of poems and songs describing the experience of being female. The songs are poetical and the poems lyrical; the line drawings whimsical yet eloquent ... selections from Sylvia Plath to Dory Previn" (Village Voice, January 27, 1975, p. 61). Illustrated by Liz Schoeberlein.

SPINGARN, Lawrence, ed. Poets West: An Anthology of Contemporary Poems from the Eleven Western States. San Rafael, Calif.: Perivale Press, 1975. 162 pp.

An above average collection including works by known and unknown poets--William Stafford, Harold Norse, etc. Biographical notes.

STANFORD, Ann, ed. The Women Poets in English: An Anthology. New York: Herder & Herder/McGraw-Hill, 1972. 374 pp.
First comprehensive collection of poetry by women from the Old English and medieval periods to the present. About 145 poets are represented--over half of them writing in the twentieth century. The introduction provides an historical overview. It is a valuable survey collection, though cramped for space. Biographical notes and indexes of authors and titles.

SUTPHEN, Dick, comp. The Sensitivity Tree. Phoenix, Ariz.: Valley of the Sun, 1972. 96 pp. Illustrated with photographs.
Biographical notes and photo of each poet accompany the selections "on life, love, and the land by six 'now' poets": Patrick Ivers, Rex Lambert, Martha McCullough, Dan Stewart, Dick Sutphen, and Henry Thome. It's the Rod McKuen school.

TAYLOR, Bruce Edward, ed. Eating the Menu: Contemporary American Poetry, 1970-1974. Dubuque, Iowa: Kendall/Hunt, 1974.

THUNDER from the Earth: A Lesbian Anthology. Chicago: Lavender Press, 1973. 32 pp. Illustrated.
"Poetry and graphics. All material by/about the lesbian lifestyle" (publisher).

TIME Pieces. Montreal: Writers' Cooperative, 1974. 114 pp.
Poetry and fiction. Eleven Canadian and American poets represented.

TIME to Greez! Incantations from the Third World. San Francisco: Third World Communications/Glide, 1975. 211 pp.
"Limited to recent works from San Francisco writers' workshops. The book is organized in sections--Aian (Asian American), Pacho che (la Raza), black, and American Indian writers. Though the materials presented are uneven in quality, a number of fine works clearly express Third World attitudes toward what they consider America's unfinished

revolution" (Library Journal, March 15, 1976, p. 820).

The TINSELTOWN Poets: A Pygmalion Anthology. Hollywood,
    Calif. : Pygmalion, 1974.
        Eight "Hollyweird" contributors: Jeff Powers, Lenore
Kouwenhoven, P. Schneidre, Rabindra, Grant Sanders, Adrian
Turcotte, Tony Perez, Fred Dorsett. Notes on poets.

TISDALE, Celes, ed. Betcha Ain't: Poems from Attica.
    Detroit: Broadside, 1974. 62 pp.
        Poems by 21 members of an Attica State Correction-
al Facility poetry workshop conducted by the editor. Editor's
ego-revealing "journal" and autobiographical statement conclude the anthology. Too much editor and not enough of the
inmates' writing, however uneven. Harold E. Packwood stands
out.

TOWNSEND, John Rowe, ed. Modern Poetry. Philadelphia:
    Lippincott, 1971. 224 pp. Illustrated with photos by
    Barbara Ffeffer.
        A sophisticated collection of more than 135 poems
by 71 modern English and American poets, intended for young
people and rewarding for adults as well. The poems are arranged roughly chronologically, beginning with the work of
poets who were young in the 1930's, and roughly grouped for
subject compatibility. The emphasis of this admittedly personal collection is on English poetry of the 60's. Indexes of
authors, first lines, and titles.

TROUPE, Quincy and Schulte, Rainer, eds. Giant Talk: An
    Anthology of Third World Writings. New York: Random,
    1975. 546 pp.
        The literature of the Third World, "the world of the
politically and economically oppressed and exploited" and those
"who identify with the historically exploited segment of man-
kind" (p. xxiii), is seen as evolving through several phases
around which the anthology is arranged: oppression and protest; violence; identity crisis; music, language, rhythm; humorous distance; ritual and magic; and conceptual voyage.
Among other international and hyphenated American writers,
the anthology includes work by more than 30 of the major
modern Black poets. The literary wealth of sections of the
"Third World" is evident, though the introduction lacks focus.
Bibliography and biographical notes.

UNTERMEYER, Louis, ed. 50 Modern American & British
    Poets, 1920-1970. New York: McKay, 1973. 358 pp.

The poets "included in this volume attained an unprecedented range and diversity" (p. xiii) and "bring clarity out
of confusion and, somehow, express the inexpressible in terms
of the unforgettable" (p. xv). The editor discusses the techniques and attitudes exemplified in modern poetry and, in the
section following the anthology, provides biographical and critical notes "meant to serve only as clues to understanding
and guides to the associations of the poetry" (p. xv). The
poets are chronologically arranged by date of birth, from
Robert Frost to Erica Jong, and are represented by two to
four poems each. Some of these poems by well known poets
have been anthologized elsewhere, and the commentaries are
aimed at uninitiated general readers or beginning students.
Still an enjoyable, rewarding collection. Index of titles and
authors. Index of first lines.

VAN DEN HEUVEL, Cor, ed. The Haiku Anthology: English
    Language Haiku by Contemporary American and Canadian
    Poets. Garden City, N. Y.: Anchor/Doubleday, 1974.
    278 pp.
        The introduction deals with definitions and forms,
haiku magazines, and the creation of standards in English.
The enjoyable collection is not restricted to poems in the 5-
7-5 format. Autobiographies.

VANGELISTI, Paul, ed. Specimen '73. Fairfax, Calif.:
    Red Hill (The Pasadena Museum of Modern Art), 1973.
        "A catalog of poets for the season 1973-74.... 12
poets from the Los Angeles basin" including work by Jack
Hirschman, Charles Bukowski, Holly Prado, Barbara Hughes,
etc. (publisher).

VAS DIAS, Robert, ed. Inside Outer Space: New Poems of
    the Space Age. Garden City, N. Y.: Anchor/Doubleday,
    1970. 440 pp.
        Good collection of 104 well and lesser known poets.
Biographical notes.

WALDMAN, Anne, ed. Another World: A Second Anthology
    of Works from the St. Mark's Poetry Project. Indiana-
    polis: Bobbs-Merrill, 1971. 387 pp.
        Selections by 77 contributors, unknown and known.
Mixed bag.

WE Are All Lesbians: A Poetry Anthology. New York: Vi-
    olet Press, 1973. 64 pp. Illustrated.
        Spirited. Fran Winant and others.

WEISHAUS, Joel, ed. <u>On the Mesa: An Anthology of Bolinas</u>
<u>Writing.</u> San Francisco: City Lights Books, 1971.
126 pp.
   "Not so much a school of poets as a meeting of those
who happen to be at this geographical location at this point in
wobbly time, several divergent movements in American poetry
of the past 20 years (Black Mountain, San Francisco Beat,
'New York School' of poets) have come together with new Western and mystic elements at the unpaved crossroads of Bo-
linas. " Fifteen contributors, including Tom Clark, Ebbe
Borregaard, and Keith Lampe, write poems, prose, scenarios.
Biographical notes.

WEISS, T. and Weiss, Renée, eds. <u>Contemporary Poetry:</u>
<u>A Retrospective from the "Quarterly Review of Literature. "</u>
Princeton, N.J. : Princeton University Press, 1974.
556 pp.
   "Poetry written during the last thirty years, culled
from the pages of one of America's foremost literary maga-
zines. ... This volume contains the work of 146 foreign and
American poets" (publisher). Clothbound edition available
from the magazine, 185 Nassau St. , Princeton, N.J. 08540.
The introduction concerns the evolution of the magazine.
Contributors are arranged alphabetically.

WEST to the Water-Six Poets: A Santa Cruz Portfolio. Lime
Kiln Press, 1972.
   "A portfolio of verse by William Everson, George
Hitchcock, Mary Norbert Korte, Peter Verblen, Naomi Clark,
and John Skinner. 200 copies, handprinted, 15 x 20 portfolio
on handmade paper, signed by the poets" (Gotham Book Mart
"Small Press Catalog 3"--price is $45. 00).

WHISNANT, Charleen and Grey, R. W. , eds. <u>Eleven Char-</u>
<u>lotte Poets.</u> Charlotte, N.C. : Red Clay Publishers,
1971. 98 pp.

WILENTZ, Ted and Weatherly, Tom. <u>Natural Process: An</u>
<u>Anthology of New Black Poetry.</u> New York: Hill and
Wang, 1970. 181 pp.
   A range of styles reflecting the concerns of Black
Americans and what has happened in Black poetry since Jones /
Baraka gained his reputation. ". . . poems that cut / like a
hawk razor. / You can't shuffle the words. " The arrangement
is alphabetical, from the work of Conyus to Al Young, and
biographies and statements by the poets are included.

YANAGI. Sausalito, Calif.: Yanagi, 1974.
     A hip, homemade venture representing 21 poets--
McClure, Clark, Meltzer, Berkson, etc.

YOUNG, Ian, ed. The Male Muse: A Gay Anthology. Tru-
     mansberg, N.Y.: Crossing Press, 1973. 127 pp.
     "Collection of poems by contemporary writers on
themes relating to male homosexuality...." Restricted to
work written by living authors in English. Not particularly
well reviewed, the criticism being that the best works have
been anthologized elsewhere and the others weren't worth
anthologizing. Forty established and less well known poets
are included. Notes on contributors.

PART 4

TEXTBOOKS

Literature textbooks, perhaps more so than the texts in many other subject areas, are important to examine since they 1) provide a conscientious representation and balance of anthologized works, and 2) include explicatory information and notes usually lacking in non-texts and of interest to both general readers and students. They are well indexed and in appearance often indistinguishable from non-texts; format, layout, feel, and visual sophistication are catching up with the competition. The competition publishes books for the trade which are often intended to be used and, in fact, find their steadiest sales in educational institutions. Textbooks, too, find their way into the general market if the packaging is right and the style is not pedantic or patronizing.

Many texts derive from a particular teaching situation and the needs of a particular student population--thus, the specialized readers appealing to the interests of young people, to ethnic concerns, etc. Others are intended as basic anthologies of all poetry of all times, usually with an emphasis on modern work.

Texts are obtainable from the publisher at a professional discount and, if a book is adopted for class use, the instructor usually gets a free copy. Free examination copies are sometimes available, but this practice is not as frequently

encountered as it used to be. Book exhibits, such as the one
at the Modern Language Association's annual conference, provide an opportunity to see what works are being published and
promoted by trade and text book publishers. Brochures, fly-
ers, and/or catalogs are available at these exhibits or can
be obtained from the publishers.

Revised editions of texts have not been included in this
list. Presumably they have already proven successful and are
widely used. Only new texts published in the 1970's which
deal with or include a good sampling of contemporary American poetry are listed and, even then, there must be some
that got away.

ABCARIAN, Richard. Words in Flight: An Introduction to
   Poetry. Belmont, Calif.: Wadsworth, 1972. 265 pp.
   Illustrated.
       The collection intends to let the poets speak for them-
selves, particularly in the first chapter, "What Is Poetry?"
The other six chapters are mini-anthologies with an illustrative purpose--"Poems for Comparison and Evaluation," for
example. The black and white and color reproductions and
poetry inspired by works of art are a unique feature of the
text. Author index and glossary.

ADAMS, William; Conn, Peter; and Slepian, Barry, eds.
   Afro-American Literature: Poetry. Boston: Houghton
   Mifflin, 1970. 130 pp.
       Collection for young adults representing 33 established
Black poets. Questions for discussion follow each poem; the
poems are arranged in nine thematic sections (The City, An-
gry Voices, etc.). Notes on the poets and index of titles and
authors.

ALLEN, John A., ed. Hero's Way: Poems in the Mythic
   Tradition. Englewood Cliffs, N.J.: Prentice-Hall, 1971.
   473 pp.
       "Contemporary poems dealing with mythic and heroic
themes" (publisher).

BACH, Bert C., Sessions, William A., and Walling, William,
   eds. The Liberating Form: A Handbook-Anthology of

English and American Poetry. New York: Dodd, Mead,
1972. 396 pp.
    "A small, highly selected anthology of English and
American poetry and a handbook on form in poetry. " Ten
sections (The Nature of Poetry, The Couplet, The Ode, etc.),
including one on Modern Poetry. Questions, Author-Title Index, Index to Critical Terms. Teacher's manual available
(publisher).

BAKER, Steward A. , ed. Ancients and Moderns: An Anthol-
    ogy of Poetry. New York: Harper & Row, 1971. 352 pp.
    "The interrelationship of form and meaning and the
importance of the reading experience are the key concepts of
this book. The poems, selected for both their sense of the
present and their student appeal, are balanced between ancients and moderns--ordered chronologically, but combined
in groups that work well together.... Major poets are extensively represented, and emphasis is given to contemporary
writers" (publisher). Intended for high school and college use.

BAYLOR, Robert and Stokes, Brenda, comps. Fine Frenzy:
    Enduring Themes in Poetry. New York: McGraw-Hill,
    1972. 417 pp.
    An ample, rewarding anthology of thematically arrang-
ed poems, very lightly annotated. The 400 poems in fifteen
sections, each arranged alphabetically, include numerous contemporary works on "Exuberance, " "Fortitude, " "Love, " "Social Problems, " etc. "A substantial teachers' manual is
available, which provides explications, teaching suggestions,
and information about records and films" (p. xxix). Author
index, glossary, and essay on prosody.

BEACHAM, E. Walton. The Meaning of Poetry: A Guide to
    Explication. Boston: Allyn and Bacon, 1974. 308 pp.

BELL, Bernard W. , ed. Modern and Contemporary Afro-
    American Poetry. Boston: Allyn and Bacon, 1972.
    193 pp.
    The editor writes that other anthologies of black po-
etry are "not adequately representative of each poet's work. "
The purpose of this anthology, including 152 poems by 29 poets from the 1920's to the 60's, is "to represent in some depth
the best modern and contemporary black American poets" with
poems revealing "the continuity and vitality of black poetry"
and providing "insight into the complex fate of being a black
American" (p. xiii). The introduction provides background
and an overview of the black literary scene aimed at students,

instructors, and general readers.   The arrangement is chronological by date of birth, from Claude McKay to Nikki Giovanni.   Poets' statements on poetics, biographical notes, selected bibliographies, lists of black presses and several little magazines, and indexes of authors and first lines are included.

BOYNTON, Robert Whitney and Mack, Maynard, comps.
   Sounds and Silences: Poems for Performing.   Rochelle
   Park, N. J. : Hayden, 1975.   114 pp.
       Geared to younger readers, "the emphasis is on stu-
dents reading poems aloud so they recognize and appreciate
the poet's dependence on, and manipulation of, normal speech
sounds and rhythms" (publisher).   The selections include work
by some moderns, including Sylvia Plath and Langston Hughes.

BRADY, Frank and Price, Martin, eds.   Poetry Past and
   Present.   New York: Harcourt Brace Jovanovich, 1974.
   527 pp.
       "A chronologically arranged anthology of 400 poems
by 115 poets--English and American--ranging from Geoffrey
Chaucer to Sylvia Plath.   With an extensive general introduction on the elements, techniques, and theories of poetry, a
detailed glossary, and an alternate thematic/generic table of
contents" (publisher).

CARLI, Angelo and Kilman, Theodore.   The Now Voices:
   The Poetry of the Present.   New York: Scribner's, 1971.
   242 pp.
       "The place to begin the study of poetry is with poems
written in the language of the reader: the student should be-
gin with poems of his own time and his own language.   Con-
sequently, the poems in this collection reflect the action,
mores, values, and social temper of this age" (p. xiv).   The
volume, which includes poems by 86 modern poets and one
computer, is divided into six sections--five thematic and one
on "The Language of Poetry. "   The title implies a hip, rous-
ing collection; this is, instead, a unique, academically solid,
meditative one with a strong connection to the '60's, and heavy
on Nemerov, Snodgrass and Lowell.   It's odd, but for the
freshmen using this book, Norman Morrison doesn't exist and
the Civil Rights Movement is history.   Indexes of poets and
poems and a glossary.

CAVANAUGH, William C. , comp.   Introduction to Poetry.
   Dubuque, Iowa: W. C. Brown, 1974.   422 (or 440) pp.

CHACE, Joan Elizabeth and Chace, William M. Making It
New. San Francisco: Canfield Press, 1973. 261 pp.
"Fifty modern poems, arranged chronologically, range
from the works of Theodore Roethke to the present 'new' poets
from the world of music. Included are lyrics by Bob Dylan,
Mick Jagger, John Lennon, Paul McCartney, Otis Redding,
Pete Seeger, and Bessie Smith" and poetry by Sam Cooke,
Bob Kaufman, Diane Wakoski, etc. (publisher).

CLAYES, Stanley A. and Gerrietts, John, eds. Ways to Poetry. New York: Harcourt Brace Jovanovich, 1975.
378 pp.
"This major new text-anthology is organized around
three ways of approaching the study of poetry: the structural,
the biographical, and the thematic. Part One, 'Elements of
Poetry,' introduces students to the fundamental methods and
techniques of the poet.... Part Two, 'Four Poets,' focuses
on the biographical relationship between the poet and the poem. It offers a substantial selection of works by each of
four poets--John Donne, William Butler Yeats, Robert Frost,
and Sylvia Plath ... arranged chronologically to indicate the
poet's artistic development. Part Three, 'Poetic Themes,'
presents poems on seven themes ... arranged chronologically.... The editors have provided commentary for each division within each part, and notes and questions for some 60
poems." Three hundred and nineteen poems in all, with a
special section on translation, Indexed. (Publisher's brochure,
including reproduction of the table of contents.)

COLLEY, Ann C. and Moore, Judith K. Starting with Poetry.
New York: Harcourt, Brace Jovanovich, 1973. 214 pp.
Illustrated.
A basic text/anthology including 180 poems "selected
for their relevance and innate appeal for today's students,"
with a concentration on contemporary poetry. "The poems
are grouped into seven sections.... Each chapter contains
several photographs that demonstrate how artists in other media perceive the same artistic elements. The first six chapters conclude with a group of poems for further reading."
An appendix titled "How to Write About Poetry" (publisher).

COLLINS, Christopher. The Act of Poetry: A Practical Introduction to the Reading of Poems. New York: Random,
1970. 320 pp.
Many contemporary examples included in a reader-
centered, eight-part text. Index of authors, titles and terms.

CONLEY, Robert J. and Cherry, Richard L. , eds. Poems
for Comparison and Contrast. New York: Macmillan,
1972. 336 pp.
Designed "primarily for the beginning student of poetry, " the poems are arranged in ten thematic units within
which poems are juxtaposed, e. g. , Whitman, Dickinson, Spender and Sandburg on trains. Not a contemporary collection--
the aim is representative historical coverage of major American and British poets--but some contemporaries are included:
Dean Deter, Ted Joans, Leroi Jones, Byron Black. Concludes
with an essay, "What to Say About a Poem, " by William K.
Wimsatt. Annotated. Index of poets with dates.

COTTER, Janet M. Invitation to Poetry. Cambridge, Mass. :
Winthrop, 1971. 377 pp. Illustrated with photographs.
"Most of the poems in this book are modern, including many written within the last ten or fifteen years ... selected for their immediacy.... the poems appear within each
section in the order which they themselves dictated, one seem-
ing to 'answer' or complement another. " The poems are divided into eight thematic sections (Portraits, Protest, etc.),
some divided further, and preceded by three chapters: "Poetry as Communication, " "Imagery and Figurative Language, "
and "The Form of Poetry. " Many of the poems are followed
by questions dealing with "experience" and "technique, " and
each section concludes with additional questions. Good selection, but the questions are perhaps more traditional than provocative. Indexes of technical terms, authors, and titles.

CRAFTS, Gretchen B. , ed. Our Own Thing: Contemporary
Thought in Poetry. Englewood Cliffs, N. J. : Prentice-
Hall, 1973. 200 pp.
Includes poems from all periods and "works of popular artists, well-known and lesser-known modern poets, and
student poets" (p. xvii). Eleven thematic sections alternating
between problem topics like "Man" and "War, " and discussions
of how poems work. The poetry is accompanied by critical
text and/or questions intended to be used by lower division
college students. Index of titles and poets and index of topics.

CUTLER, Charles L. and others, eds. Now Poetry. Mid-
dletown, Conn. : Xerox Education Publications 1971.
63 pp. Illustrated.
A booklet for elementary school students, describing
several ways of making poems (concrete, impressionistic,
etc.) with examples, mainly by young people.

DeFORD, Sara and Lott, Clarinda H.   Forms of Verse: British and American.   New York: Appleton-Century-Crofts,
   1971.   392 pp.

EVANS, David Allan, ed.   New Voices in American Poetry:
   An Anthology.   Cambridge, Mass. : Winthrop, 1973.
   265 pp.   Illustrated with photos of the contributors.
      "The combination of poetry and critiques by the poets
   is ... expecially appropriate for courses in creative writing
   ... [and] contemporary poetry.   The book is not, however,
   intended exclusively as a textbook ... [or] as a definitive selection of poems by new or young American poets" (p. iv).
   Eclectic, wide-ranging representation of the work of 45 poets
   arranged alphabetically from James Applewhite to Al Young.
   Photos, biographical notes, and, in most cases, intriguing
   essays or notes by the poets on one or more of the selections
   are included.

GELPI, Albert Joseph, ed.   The Poet in America: 1650 to
   the Present.   Lexington, Mass. : Heath, 1973.   839 pp.
   Illustrated.
      Divided into four sections: Colonial Beginnings,
   American Romantic Poetry, The American Poetic Renaissance,
   and The Contemporary Scene.   Ample selections by each poet,
   arranged chronologically by date of birth.   The fourth section
   includes 22 poets ranging from Theodore Roethke to Denise
   Levertov to Al Young.   Introductions, biographical notes,
   footnotes, and bibliographies.

GIBB, Carson.   Exposition and Literature.   New York: Macmillan, 1971.   260 pp.
      A two-part college text setting forth, in the first
   part, principles of exposition and, in the second, an essay on
   reading poetry.   Examples are quoted to illustrate the elements of poetry.   Glossary of literary terms and index.

GRAVES, Barbara Farris and McBain, Donald J.   Lyric Voices:
   Approaches to the Poetry of Contemporary Song.   New
   York: Wiley, 1972.   208 pp.
      An attempt to put the lyric phenomenon "in some kind
   of a poetic and cultural perspective" for use in an introductory
   poetry course, in a seminar on the lyric, or as a supplementary text.   Twenty-eight poet-singers are represented (Paul
   Simon, Bob Dylan, etc.).   If this is the text in a course, the
   students will be shortchanged as far as poetry goes, but the
   study questions do force a deeper look at what people are

hearing and responding to in popular music circles; still, this
approach will become historical rather than contemporary as
yesterday's hits become golden oldies. Supplemental reading
list, discography, and index to authors, titles and first lines.

HALL, Donald, ed. The Pleasures of Poetry. New York:
     Harper, 1971. 338 pp. Record.
        "The editor's introductory critical essays present a
view of poetry free from the strictures of old approaches and
'new criticism.' Part II contains several poems by 'Ten
Great Poets'.... Part III presents 'One Hundred Great English Poems' by a wide variety of poets. Part IV contains
five Beatles' lyrics" (publisher).

HAMILTON, Horace. The Cage of Form: Likeness and Dif-
     ference in Poetry. Encino, Calif.: Dickenson, 1972.
     280 pp.
        A solid, thoughtful text with no special affinity for
the contemporary (the Beats, for example, are disparaged),
more suitable for those with prior interest. The eight chapters deal with topics such as "Metaphor and Meaning" and
"The Poem in its Context" and conclude with exercises titled
"Practical Criticism." Glossary. Index.

HARLAN, William K. Probes: An Introduction to Poetry.
     New York: Macmillan, 1973. 388 pp. Illustrated.
        A two-color, illustrated, and typographically varied
text with a contemporary emphasis, concluding with the sug-
gestion to PRESS HERE since "The end of a textbook is self-
destruction." Intended for media-oriented, uninitiated students. The format may be confusing and crowded, but it
won't put anyone to sleep. Index of Poets and Titles, Index
of First Lines, Author Index (arranged by page number since
attribution doesn't accompany the works anthologized).

The HEATH Introduction to Poetry. Preface and a brief his-
     tory by Joseph de Roche. Lexington, Mass.: Heath,
     1975. 480 pp. (est.).
        "This chronologically arranged anthology of English,
American, and Canadian poetry offers a wide range of works
representative of every period, but with special emphasis on
the twentieth century. A general introduction provides an
overview of the technical elements of poetry.... An Appendix
includes a glossary of poetic terms, an index of authors and
titles, and an index of first lines" (publisher).

HOGAN, Homer. Poetry of Relevance. Toronto: Methuen,

1970. 2 vols. Illustrated with photos.
"Each song lyric is followed by one or more poems
that develop the theme or poetic technique found in the lyric....
Contemporary Canadian, British and American poetry accounts
for about half the poems. " The volumes have introductions
relating to the experience and interpretations of literature,
descriptive material, discographies, indexes of themes and
poets and songwriters, suggestions for study, and brief critical biographies of the poets. An exciting text intended for
secondary school students.

HOGINS, James Burl, comp. Literature: Poetry. Chicago:
     Science Research Associates, 1973. 360 pp.
          Comprehensive anthology with brief explications and
study questions. Glossary and index.

HUNTER, J. Paul, ed. Poetry: The Norton Introduction to
     Literature. New York: Norton, 1973. 573 pp.
          The preface describes how to read a poem and "ask
the right questions. " The 624 annotated poems (over half
from the twentieth century, with the emphasis on recent work)
are arranged in groups to invite comparison, later groups
becoming more sophisticated. Included are "enjoyable, stim-
ulating, and significant literary works, " familiar and unfamiliar, some occasional poetry, lyrics, Black poetry, and works
based on nonwestern traditions. A longer supplement on
Adrienne Rich is included, in addition to ten short essays
which discuss technical problems and define terms. List of
terms, index of authors, and index of titles and first lines.

HURTIK, Emil and Yarber, R. E. , comps. An Introduction
     to Poetry and Criticism. New York: Xerox College,
     1972. 254 pp.

JACOBUS, Lee A. and Moynihan, William T. , eds. Poems
     in Context. New York: Harcourt Brace Jovanovich,
     1974. 524 pp.
          "Introduces students to the study of poetry by inviting
them to consider a poem from a wide range of critical perspectives.... organized around the distinction between the
internal contexts of language ... and the external contexts. "
The text contains about 350 poems from a wide range of historical periods and study questions interspersed throughout.
An Instructor's Manual accompanies the text (publisher).

KEHL, Delmar G. Poetry and the Visual Arts. Belmont,
     Calif. : Wadsworth, 1975. Approx. 256 pp. Illustrated.

"Thirty-nine poetry-visual art sets; each set contains reproductions of one or more works of visual art and a poem or poems based upon or related to the art," such as "Before an Old Painting of the Crucifixion" by N. Scott Momaday and the Mission Carmel Painting of the Crucifixion. Commentaries, suggestions for discussion and writing, glossary, bibliography, additional poem-visual art sets. Instructor's manual available (publisher).

KENNEDY, X. J., ed.   Introduction to Poetry.   Boston: Little, Brown, 1971.

_____.   Messages: A Thematic Anthology of Poetry.
Boston: Little, Brown, 1973.   386 pp.
A unique feature of this anthology: to avoid distraction from the meaning and message, the poets' names appear at the end of the book rather than bylining each poem. Glossary and notes on the poets with bibliography and discography for each.

KOPPELL, Kathleen Sunshine.   Live Poetry.   New York: Holt, Rinehart and Winston, 1971.   196 pp.   Illustrated with photographs.
"Over 125 poems and lyrics [by 68 poets and singers], most written during the past fifteen years. They attack the most important of contemporary concerns in contemporary language" (p. xiii). The poets, many of whom are women, represent diverse backgrounds, minority groups, and different generations. Some are established names; some are younger and not yet well known. The selections are arranged alphabetically by author's name. A separate guidebook to the anthology is available.

LAPIDES, Frederick R. and Shawcross, John T.   Poetry and Its Conventions: An Anthology Examining Poetic Forms and Themes.   New York: Free Press, 1972.   552 pp.
"We have attempted to present the traditional poetic forms and conventions, and we have tried to show how these genres and conventions developed, how they have been used, how they have undergone modifications, and how they are used today in poetry" (p. xxvii). The emphasis is on the heritage of the past as it relates to the present and the quoted examples are drawn mainly from the classics of the past. The text and anthologized work are divided into six parts according to form, style, and theme (e.g., "The Lyric" and "The Poem as Drama"). The poetry is annotated and there is a glossary of poetical and critical terms and author, title and first-line indexes.

McMICHAEL, James L. and Saleh, Dennis, eds. Just What
the Country Needs, Another Poetry Anthology. Belmont,
Calif. : Wadsworth, 1971. 191 pp.
The newest work of 30 American poets including Gary
Snyder, W. S. Merwin, Philip Levine, etc. , and several
younger poets never before anthologized. Biographical notes
(publisher).

MARSHALL, Carol, comp. Twentieth Century Poetry.
(Houghton Books in Literature: Kenneth S. Lynn, Advis-
ing Editor) New York: Houghton, 1971. 180 pp. Illustrated.

MECKLENBURGER, James A. and Simmons, Gary. Since
Feeling Is First. Glenview, Ill. : Scott, Foresman and
Co. , 1971. 190 pp. Illustrated.
"A visual and poetic montage of the many emotions,
sensitivities, and concerns of young adults, this introductory
poetry anthology is designed to draw the student into the experience of poetry. Over 200 poems, predominantly modern, are combined with visuals.... Themes of war, love,
education, and religion interweave and interact ... " (publisher).

MILLER, J. E. and others. Lyric Potential: Arrangements
and Techniques in Poetry. Glenview, Ill. : Scott, Foresman and Co. , 1974.
Intended for high school use.

MILLER, Ruth, ed. Blackamerican Literature: 1760-Present.
Beverly Hills, Calif. : Glencoe Press, 1971. 774 pp.
A comprehensive collection including slave naratives,
plays, essays, orations, excerpts from novels and autobiographies, and poetry. Selections by eighteen poets writing
between 1940-1963 and from 1963 to the present, plus several
pages of Clarence Major's introduction to The New Black Poetry (New York: International Publishers, 1969), are included.
Time lines, author index, bibliography.

MONACO, Richard, ed. New American Poetry. New York:
McGraw-Hill, 1973. 184 pp. Photos of poets.
Anthology weighted toward the New York School.
Nineteen contributors including Richard Kostelanetz, Clark
Coolidge, and Karen Swenson. Biographical notes.

_____. and Briggs, John, eds. The Logic of Poetry.
With Notes on Prosody by Christopher Collins. New
York: McGraw-Hill, 1974. 428 pp. Illustrated.

Three hundred and ten poems (100 of which are modern), organized around the concept of poetic metaphor. Glossary of critical terms (publisher).

MONTAGUE, Gene. <u>Poetry and a Principle</u>. Philadelphia: Lippincott, 1972. 312 pp.
The principle is that "Meaning results from a juxtaposition of the expected with the unexpected" (p. 2). Wide-ranging, good selection of poetry and informative text illustrating the "principle" and divided into eight chapters. About one-third of the poems are discussed as examples of a particular technique, form, etc.; about one-third are followed by questions for discussion; and one-third are included for study and accompanied, in some cases, by questions and annotations. Index of author, title and first lines and index of terms and a glossary.

NIMS, John Frederick. <u>Western Wind: An Introduction to Poetry</u>. New York: Random, 1974. 466 pp. Illustrated.
Over 300 poems with an emphasis on modern and contemporary poetry arranged under seven categories (The Senses, The Words, The Mind, etc.) divided into 23 chapters, the last titled "Poems Without Voice: Concrete and Other." The text looks at poetry as "an expression of our human experience" (p. xvii) and relates it to the other arts and sciences. A well written and sophisticated work intended for college classes at the elementary or advanced levels. The first 16 chapters provide the basics, and the other seven "go more deeply into the nature of poetry" (p. xix). Exercises conclude each chapter. Index of authors and titles and indexes of first lines, terms, and alternate index.

PERKINS, George, ed. <u>American Poetic Theory</u>. New York: Holt, Rinehart & Winston, 1972. 383 pp.
A collection of "statements that American poets have made on the theory and practice of their craft." Among the moderns: Ginsberg, Creeley, Bly, and Dickey (publisher).

PERRY, John Oliver. <u>The Experience of Poems: A Text and Anthology</u>. New York: Macmillan, 1972. 587 pp.
Introduction deals with why and how we read and discuss poems. The following five sections deal with topics such as "Voice and Tone" and "Particularities of Language and Form in Poems," broken down into chapters which define terms, forms, etc. and explicate particular poems. The anthology consists of a wide range of poetry from Milton and King David to contempories Ginsberg, Jones/Baraka, etc.,

arranged in alphabetical order. A rigorous and detailed text,
mainly for those with prior interest. Index to authors, titles
and first lines and index to critical terms.

PICHASKE, David R. , ed. Beowulf to Beatles: Approaches
    to Poetry. New York: Free Press, 1972. 410 pp.
        "This book accepts the idea of a poetry of rock and
uses that poetry in conjunction with the poetry traditionally
taught in poetry courses" (p. xxvi). It is planned to move
from author analysis to reader analysis, and the final chapter
is a thematically arranged anthology without editorial comment.
The selections "favor the contemporary, the fresh, and the
profane. " The seven chapters divided into 35 sections cover
genre, technique, theme, and contain questions for study.
List of recordings, bibliography, and index of title and authors.

PIERCE, Barbara B. and Pierce, Robert B. The Design of
    Poetry. (Pendulum Literature Series: Lawrence Buell,
    series editor) West Haven, Conn. : Pendulum Press,
    1973. 80 pp.
        A brief, dry lesson on persona, imagery, symbolism,
etc. The concluding chapter, "Writing a Poetic Analysis, "
is uninspiring. Glossary.

PILON, A. Barbara, ed. Concrete Is Not Always Hard.
    Middletown, Conn. : Xerox Education Publications, 1972.
    96 pp.
        A collection of word play and concrete poems, with
introductory notes for elementary school students and teachers. In most of these works form outweighs content, stimu-
lating, perhaps, artifice rather than feeling in the students'
own creative efforts.

PINNEY, Wilson G. , ed. Two Ways of Seeing: An Anthology
    of Poems and Photos. Boston: Little, Brown, 1971.
    208 pp. Illustrated with photos by Allen Say.

POULIN, A. Jr, ed. Contemporary American Poetry. Bos-
    ton: Houghton Mifflin, 1971; second ed. , 1975. 512 pp.
    Illustrated with photos of the poets.
        "Features notes on the poets, a general critical es-
say dealing with the trends in American poetry since 1945, a
bibliography of criticism.... For undergraduate courses"
(publisher).

RAFFEL, Burton, ed. Introduction to Poetry. New York:
    New American Library, 1971. 160 pp.

_____. Poems: An Anthology. New York: New Ameri-
can Library, 1971. 224 pp.
          Companion volumes with the collection and discussion
ranging over various periods and styles. Annotated (publisher).

RICHARDSON, H. Edward and Shroyer, Frederick B. Muse
     of Fire: Approaches to Poetry. New York: Knopf,
     1971. 314 (+ 51) pp. Illustrated with photographs.
          "Introduction to the basic techniques, criticism, and--
most especially--the verities and delights of poetry. " Part
One (76 pages) consists of nine chapters on various approaches
to poetry--romantic, sociocultural, psychological, etc. The
concluding chapter, "Synthesis of Approaches, " revolves
around Yeats' "The Second Coming, " demonstrating "that critical schools need not necessarily be mutually exclusive. "
Part Two is an anthology "of which around 70 per cent is relatively modern, and the rest drawn from earlier twentieth-
century decades and preceding centuries, " grouped under fourteen thematic headings and arranged "in each section in reverse chronological order" (p. xv). Explanatory notes and
questions for study conclude each section. A separate section, "The Basics of Poetry, " deals with form, structure,
technique, etc. Fine text and anthology offering more balance
and substance than most. Indexes to the text, the poets, the
poems, and poetic terms (with pronunciation guide), and a
glossary.

ROSS, Robert H. and Stafford, William E. Poems and Per-
     spectives. Glenview, Ill. : Scott, Foresman and Co. ,
     1971. 633 pp.
          "Anthology of poetry with a full historical and analyt-
ical sequence of critical prose pieces that illuminate the poetry. The first part of the book is a collection of the best
in English and American poetry, with a predominance of modern works.... The critical section offers some of literature's most significant prose comments, analyses, and real-
izations about the poems and poetry. As in the poetry section, full regard is given to established landmarks, but most
selections reflect the modern literary scene" (publisher).

RYLANDER, John D. and Rylander, Edith. What's in a Po-
     em. Encino, Calif. : Dickenson, 1972.
          "Introduction to poetry ... through discussion and in-
novative exercises. " Poets from all times are represented
in an anthology divided into nine sections: Rhyme, Diction,
Free Verse and Self-Devised Forms, etc. (publisher). Index of poetic terms. Index of authors and titles.

SALINAS, Luis Omar and Faderman, Lillian. From The
    Barrio: A Chicano Anthology. San Francisco: Can-
    field Press, 1973. 154 pp.
        The authors included "are Chicanos concerned with
Chicanismo, both as a political stand and as a life style" (p.
vi). The collection is divided into two parts: "My Revolution" (political statements) and "My House" (personal statements). Each part contains a poetry section--36 poems by
11 poets. Fine, moving selection including autobiographical
notes.

SCHMITTROTH, John and Mahoney, John, eds. New Poets,
    New Music. Cambridge, Mass.: Winthrop, 1970. 106
    pp. Illustrated with photos.
        An effort to get students into poetry through the top
ten, but already dated for its au courant intention. Lyrics
by composer-poets Judy Collins, Joni Mitchell, Laura Nyro,
Paul Simon, etc. An introduction, five short essays, and a
selected discography are included.

SOMER, John and Cozzo, Joseph. Poetic Experience: Public
    Poems and Private Visions. Glenview, Ill.: Scott, Fores-
    man and Co., 1970. 192 pp.
        "The public poems and private visions of the British
and American poets gathered in this collection exemplify the
major forms of poetic expression. The 179 poems included
represent the prominent periods in the development of poetry
and the dominant themes within each period. The modern selections include experimental as well as more conventional
works. Containing an alternate table of contents which lends
itself to five different approaches to poetry: Historical, thematic, formal, major writers, and poetic modes. An index
of first lines is included" (publisher).

STEIN, A. The Uses of Poetry. New York: Holt, Rinehart
    & Winston, 1975.

SUGG, Richard P. Appreciating Poetry. Boston: Houghton
    Mifflin, 1975. 352 pp.
        "Approaches poetry structurally, thematically, and
chronologically. Includes introductions, questions, glossaries,
and bibliographies" (publisher). Sixty-four page instructor's
manual is available.

SWANGER, David. The Poem as Process. New York: Har-
    court Brace Jovanovich, 1973. 256 pp.
        "A theoretical exposition of the problems of poetic

response, with stress on the actual writing of poems and a detailed discussion of the creative process. " The six chapters include discussion of some 50 poems and rock lyrics, and an anthology of 50 additional poems concludes the book (publisher).

SWEETKIND, Morris, comp. Getting into Poetry. Boston: Holbrook Press, 1972. 387 pp.

TAYLOR, Henry, comp. Poetry: Points of Departure. Englewood Cliffs, N. J. : Prentice-Hall, 1974. 345 pp.

THOMAS, D. M. Poetry in Crosslight. New York: Longman, 1975. Illustrated.

THOMPSON, Ruth and Thompson, Marvin, comps. The Total Experience of Poetry: An Introductory Anthology. New York: Random House, 1970. 264 pp.

TREVOR, J. Robert and Zall, Paul. Proverb to Poem. New York: McGraw-Hill, 1970. 320 pp.
        "This introduction to literature focuses on those elements considered essential to the understanding of fiction and poetry from the casual reader's point of view.... The text is organized around checkpoints--questions a student should ask himself before and after reading a short story or poem" (publisher). Glossary of poetic terms.

TURCO, Lewis. Poetry: An Introduction Through Writing. Reston, Va. : Reston (Prentice-Hall), 1973. 406 pp.
        "Meant to introduce college students to the genre of poetry from the writer's point-of-view, by presenting them with the same problems that aspiring poets encounter ... " (p. xiii). The book deals with method, form, structure and the language of poetry (prosodies, poetic voices, and genres); intended for students with prior interest and tested in practice at SUNY-Oswego. It includes numerous definitions with examples, writing exercises, and explications of the formal techniques discernible in some of the poetry quoted. Many of the author's own works are included, as are works by major poets of this and other centuries, in a wide-ranging selection of high caliber. The test is useful for poets and critics, but as for helping people write and enjoy poetry, it's not the answer--unless form is your preoccupation. Three-book bibliography and lengthy index.

WERTHEIM, Bill and Gonzales, Irma, eds. Talkin' About Us:

Writings by Students in the Upward Bound Program. New York: Meredith, 1970. 176 pp.
Poems and stories in five thematically arranged sections by participants in the nationwide Upward Bound Program. The collection is intended to be used as a supplementary text in college and high school English classes. The editors favored writing in a natural idiom about issues meaningful to young adults. Uneven.

WILLIAMS, Miller, ed. Contemporary Poetry in America. New York: Random, 1973. 189 pp. Photos of the poets.
A chronologically arranged anthology of 96 poets, born in the twentieth century, who gained a reputation after World War II. It is a handsome oversized paperback providing an overview of contemporary poetry with supplemental bibliographies for each poet, autobiographical notes, a listing of records, and indexes of poets and poems. Content and format will appeal to a wide audience.

WINKLER, Anthony C. Poetry as System. Glenview, Ill.: Scott, Foresman and Co., 1971. 259 pp.
The focus is "on the machinery implicit in each poem." Poetry is divided into "three conceptual models": the object poem, the abstraction poem and the speaker-as-object poem. Within this structure, poems from various periods, with an emphasis on modern poetry, are discussed (though the interpretations are not always the only interpretation). Abstract, concrete, and underground poetry are covered in a separate chapter on modern poetry. Four chapters conclude with poems for further study in addition to an anthology at the end of the book, adding up to a total of 108 poems. Among the longer works are Ginsberg's "Howl," the first book of Williams' "Patterson," and Olson's "letters" from "The Maximus Poems." The appendix contains Olson's "Projective Verse," a glossary, and "Position 1 of the International Movement." This is a well done introduction to poetry and a thoughtfully selected anthology intended for use in literature and creative writing courses. Index of poems and authors.

TOPICAL GUIDE

AFRO-AMERICAN

AFRO-AMERICAN (cont'd)

AMERICAN INDIAN

ASIAN AMERICAN

CANADIAN

CHRISTIAN

CONCRETE

GAY

TEACHING (EXCLUDING TEXTBOOKS)

AUTHOR INDEX

Abcarian, Richard, 82
Abdul, Raoul, 46, 65
Adams, William, 82
Adoff, Arnold, 46
Algarin, Miguel, 77
Alix, 47
Allen, Donald, 18, 35
Allen, John A. , 82
Allen, Terry D. , 47
Altick, Richard D. , 4
American Center of P. E. N. ,
13
Anderson, Douglas, 18
Angoff, Charles, 48
Arata, Esther Spring, 12
Atkinson, Bob, 48
Atlas, James, 48

Bach, Bert C. , 82
Bailey, Leaonead Pack, 11
Baker, Jeffrey A. , 9
Baker, Steward A. , 83
Balazs, Mary Webber, 60
Baloian, James, 61
Barba, Sharon, 51
Barry, Jan, 73
Bass, Ellen, 59
Baylor, Robert, 83
Beacham, E. Walton, 83
Beck, Dorothy, 48
Bell, Bernard W. , 19, 83
Bell, Inglis R. , 3
Blackburn, G. Meredith, 7
Bloom, Harold, 19
Bogan, Louise, 20
Bonazzi, Robert, 48

Bowles, Jerry G. , 49
Boyd, Gertrude A. , 20
Boyers, Robert, 20
Boynton, Robert Whitney,
84
Bradbury, Malcolm, 15
Brady, Frank, 84
Breman, Paul, 49
Brewton, John E. , 7
Brewton, Sarah W. , 7
Briggs, John, 91
Brooks, Cleanth, 20
Brooks, Gwendolyn, 20,
49, 50
Bruchac, Joseph, 20, 50
Bruns, Gerald L. , 21
Buchler, Justus, 21
Bukowski, Charles, 50
Bulkin, Elly, 50
Burnshaw, Stanley, 21
Bush, Terri, 61

Cargas, Harry J. , 21
Carli, Angelo, 84
Carruth, Hayden, 50
Cavanaugh, William C. , 84
Chace, Joan Elizabeth, 85
Chace, William M. , 85
Chandler, Sue P. , 11
Chapman, Abraham, 50
Chapman, Dorothy, H. , 8
Charters, Samuel, 22
Chase, John Terry, 57
Chatfield, Hale, 22
Cherry, Neeli, 50
Cherry, Richard L. , 86

109

TITLE INDEX

115